# FAMOUS WOMEN
# TENNIS PLAYERS

# FAMOUS WOMEN TENNIS PLAYERS

### by Trent Frayne

ILLUSTRATED WITH PHOTOGRAPHS

Dodd, Mead & Company · New York

Library of Congress Cataloging in Publication Data

Frayne, Trent.
  Famous women tennis players.

  1. Women tennis players—Biography.   I. Title.
GV994.A1F72      796.34'2'0922[B]        78-22428
ISBN 0-396-07681-5

To June, again

# CONTENTS

# FAMOUS WOMEN
# TENNIS PLAYERS

*Suzanne Lenglen*

# SUZANNE LENGLEN

## [1899–1938]

No ONE CHANGED the face of women's tennis the way Suzanne Lenglen did, not even Billie Jean King who came along four decades later leading a revolution.

God help the girl who wanted to swing a racquet in public in the days before La Belle Lenglen, the Parisienne who become known wherever the game was played as the Maid Marvel of France. Lenglen had a style and a verve and a panache and a skill that did for women's tennis what the dashing and aristocratic Bill Tilden did for men's. But she was revered for more than this by onlookers and a great deal more by contemporaries.

"All women tennis players should go on their knees in thankfulness to Suzanne for delivering them from the tyranny of corsets," sighed Elizabeth Ryan, the American doubles star who won the first of her nineteen Wimbledon titles in 1914.

The way women used to dress to play the game is damned nearly terrifying. Back in 1912 Mrs. Lambert Chambers, who dominated Edwardian tennis, would totter across the lawns wearing three stiff petticoats, long-sleeved blouses with collars and cuffs and sometimes even neckties. Once, a few years earlier, the Californian May Sutton precipitated a widespread outbreak of indignation at Wimbledon not just by appearing in one of her father's shirts instead of the traditional blouses but by rolling back the cuffs and revealing bared wrists.

Clothing caused the players far more discomfort and pain than their opponents ever did. Bloodied underclothing was not the least uncommon as the wire stays of corsets dug into the flesh of players straining on the courts. "Hearty indeed would be the thanks of puzzled lady players to the individual who invented an easy and pretty costume," wrote Lottie Dod in 1905. Lottie was one of England's most famous players at the turn of the century. She had won her first Wimbledon championship at the age of fifteen in 1887 wearing calf-length skirts, and she was able to get away with this heresy because she was a schoolgirl in her school uniform. When Lottie Dod grew older she was compelled to climb into ground-length skirts like everyone else.

In 1919 at the end of World War I when tennis resumed at Wimbledon, along came the magnificent Suzanne, then aged twenty, wickedly daring in a flimsy one-piece cotton frock of calf-length with short sleeves and—great Gods of fire!—*no petticoats.*

"In 1920 Suzanne returned with the new bobbed hair style," the dress designer Ted Tinling wrote in recollection. "She swathed her head in several yards of brightly colored silk chiffon and the 'Lenglen Bandeau,' as it was called, swept through every conceivable area of fashion. Likewise, the Lenglen one-piece frock was almost universally adopted for everyday wear. Later she induced the top Paris couturiers to design for her, and she introduced the first silk dresses to tennis. Over these she wore hip-length silk cardigans, matching her bandeaux. She frequently played in shiny white silk stockings rolled to the knee, and in cool weather she often went to court in a lavish fur coat on which she'd pinned an admirer's flower corsage."

Suzanne Lenglen's place in tennis is not confined entirely to the look of her well-turned calf, however. She is also, arguably, the woman whose name belongs at the head of the all-time list of performers—ahead of Helen Wills, ahead of Billie Jean, ahead, even, of Christ Evert who threatened to make the game her very own in the middle 1970s. Time and technique and improved equipment produced progressively more powerful performers, perhaps, but champions in any sphere are judged according to the competition and conditions of the day, and in this area Lenglen was supreme. She won the first of her six Wimbledon championships when she was twenty in 1919, and each year added the women's doubles championship partnered by Elizabeth Ryan. She joined three men, G. L. Patterson, Jean Borotra and Peter O'Hara Wood, in winning three mixed doubles titles there. No one could touch her in the French championships in the six years of her dominance of tennis, and there seems no question that her list of championships would have been considerably longer had she not been a victim of chronic illness—she died at thirty-nine of leukemia—that frequently threatened her career and often compelled her to default matches and sometimes tournaments. In 1924, for instance, an attack of jaundice kept her out of the French Championships, and although she undertook to defend her title at Wimbledon that year doctors advised her to withdraw halfway through. She took a long rest at Nice and returned to the courts with a renewed flair in 1925. In Paris she won her fifth French title, then descended triumphantly upon Wimbledon and won her sixth singles championship, the doubles with Elizabeth Ryan and the mixed with Borotra.

No question about it, Wimbledon was Suzanne's cup of tea—as it was Tilden's in the first half of the decade of the 1920s.

"The appearance on the Wimbledon scene of Suzanne Lenglen from France and Bill Tilden from the U.S. just after the First World War brought to the game an undreamed of popularity," Roy McKelvie wrote fifty years later. In the mid-1970s McKelvie looked back from his office in the All-England tennis club at Wimbledon on a long career as a journalist, author and press officer, a brisk, robust, red-faced veteran with a thatch of white curly hair and a manner to scare hell out of any of the hundreds of journalists who attend Wimbledon each summer and might wander onto the scene with improper credentials. McKelvie continues:

> There were queues stretching from Worple Road, the original site of the club, to Wimbledon Station to watch Suzanne play. Worple Road was not large enough to accommodate the crowds. So, in 1922, Wimbledon moved to its present site in Church Road. When Suzanne made her first appearance there, on the first Wednesday, people began queuing in the early hours of the morning. The sight was described as the
>
> *'Leng-len trail a-winding.'*

It was the personalities of these two players as much as their skill that attracted people and the moment when tennis became not just a game to play but one to enjoy as if it were theatre. The personality cult is stronger today though not even Ilie Nastase, Bjorn Borg, Rod Laver and others stand out to quite the same extent as did the Queen from France and the Giant from the United States.

Concomitant with the rise of personalities came the gossip, tittle-tattle and newspaper stories of what goes on behind the scenes. Tilden's apparent dislike and contempt for Mlle. Lenglen and Jean Borotra; the alleged feud between Helen Wills and Helen Jacobs made headlines as big as any of those achieved by Nastase's antics on court, rows with players and officials.

Tilden, perhaps inspired by jealousy, once said of Mlle. Lenglen that she combined the characteristics of a streetwalker and a prima donna. Shortly before she met the American Molla Mallory at Forest Hills, Tilden humiliated the French lady by beating her with hardly the loss of a point, and then announcing that she would lose to the American. In fact, suffering from whooping cough, Suzanne retired to Mrs. Mallory after losing the first set 6–2.

Some years later, Tilden relented and in a reflective mood described Suzanne as a unique personality with an individuality and magnetism that held the public interest. He wrote: 'She was the biggest drawing card in the tennis world'.

Here we have the essence of Lenglen, this enormous attractiveness. There was something seductively compelling about this woman whose features never were described as beautiful but whose movement, poise and vibrant personality dominated any setting. There was much of the grand-opera diva about her—the dramatic nature of her clothes and makeup, the tantrums and near swoons, the inescapable theatricality of her presence.

She was an only child of doting though highly ambitious parents. She was born at Compiègne on May 24, 1899—her name is always associated with the south of France, with Nice and the Côte d'Azur, but these places came later. When her father saw her dominate other girls on the tennis courts through a natural flair for the game, he invested time in the careful instruction of his tiny, sallow-complexioned daughter. At fourteen Suzanne won both women's singles and doubles in the World Hard Court championships in Paris, and a year later before the onslaught of World War I she scored a surprise by beating Elizabeth Ryan at Cannes. Because of the war, her debut at Wimbledon was delayed until 1919. Obviously her skill would have had her there long before.

The Lenglen family—pére, mére and Suzanne—had moved to Nice in 1912, by chance settling near the home of the Ballet Russe de Monte Carlo. Perhaps it was watching young ballerinas in their arduous training that influenced Suzanne's balletic style of play on the tennis courts, and perhaps the style of her clothes as well.

The accuracy of her shots caught the eye as quickly as the grace of her movement. This accuracy was the result of the training her father had given her at Nice. There, he'd place coins on the court as targets, a drill that sharpened the placement of her shots and her concentration. Her father dwelled on the importance of proper footwork in getting into position to stroke the ball properly.

With all of this, by the time Suzanne Lenglen was thirteen Mediterranean tourists were becoming aware of her burgeoning reputation, and they returned to London and Boston and New York with excited accounts of the new star emerging in France.

By 1919, then, Wimbledon galleries were anticipating her appearance keenly. But when she arrived, head high and smiling, at centre court in her one-piece dress, her skirt at mid-calf and her arms bared, they found her appearance shocking and well-nigh indecent. Suzanne was impervious to the widespread criticism; indeed, in 1920 she wore makeup and appeared with short hair wrapped in a yard or more of silk. She wore numerous shades of silk, usually in colors that she could coordinate with her lipstick and her frocks. The headpieces, which became celebrated internationally as "the Lenglen Bandeaux" took the fashion salons by storm, as popular away from tennis courts as on them, and were adapted by women everywhere with no interest or knowledge of tennis.

And Suzanne was really just beginning. Subsequently at Wimbledon she wore silk stockings under her calf-length skirts and made magnificent entrances onto the court, wrapped in clinging furs, or in coats with tall fur collars. No question about it, she was something.

None of this could have been of more than passing moment, it seems likely, had she not been so dominant a force once the matches began. She seemed incapable of an awkward movement, her body and grace as fascinating as those of the most glowing ballerinas. She never seemed to scramble or stumble or be caught off balance, and she always seemed in position to stroke the ball properly, keeping her opponents so deep against the baseline that they couldn't trap her with sharply angled shots but could only hurry back and forth from sideline to sideline to retrieve Lenglen's endless depth.

In almost no time Lenglen was turning the legend of

17

the precocious teenager into the reality of the mature young woman. In her first Wimbledon she rushed through to the final round to oppose the defending champion, Dorothea Lambert Chambers, seeking her seventh Wimbledon championship.

They engaged in a dramatic match, one involving the champion's steady ground strokes and the young French woman's rounded game of serve, drive, volley and smash. Lenglen pulled out the strenuous first set by 10–8, then fell behind at 1–4 in the second. She came back at this critical stage to 4–4. Chambers should have folded at this point. She had won the 1914 Wimbledon a few months before World War I closed down the tournament for five years, so that by 1919 she was forty-one. A defending champion at that time did not participate in the championship draw but waited as an automatic finalist for an opponent to emerge from the draw as a challenger. Nonetheless, tied at 4–4 and down a set and playing in her first truly serious match in five years, Chambers won the next two games to win the set and level the match.

Now it was Lenglen's turn to rush ahead on a 4–1 lead and be overhauled. Indeed, Chambers seemed destined to defend the crown successfully, leading 6–5 and 40–15 and serving two match points. Here, with unflinching nerves, Lenglen held nothing back on her next series of shots and, gauging them perfectly, won four points in a row. That rally pulled out the game and tied the set at 6–6. Lenglen got ahead again in the next game and, amazingly, Chambers summoned the resources of a champion to deadlock the match once more. But at 7–7 that was her last hurrah. Lenglen won the next two games and, with them, the match at 10–8, 4–6, 9–7.

In 1920 the remarkably agile Englishwoman and the lithe star who was more than twenty years her junior returned to Wimbledon, only now Lenglen as the defending champion waited in the wings for a challenger and Chambers played through the draw, hoping for a rematch in front of the royal box.

She did emerge too, but this time she met a player who had prospered enormously with an added year of experience, one now equipped with a more sustained accuracy and even keener anticipation. Lenglen didn't give the English player a chance. Movingly easily, always in position, she dashed off the first set with loss of three games and in the second dropped none.

And while retaining the one-piece dress, drawn at the waist with a band of ribbon and with a pleated skirt, the Maid Marvel of France now replaced a soft linen hat of 1919 with the dash of the Lenglen Bandeau that was to set a new international pattern for women faced with the towering question of the ages: What will I do with my hair?

In 1921 in a third appearance at Wimbledon and still unbeaten anywhere in the three years since the end of the war, Lenglen was challenged by her first American finalist opponent, Elizabeth Ryan. The match loomed as a test for Suzanne when each woman held service through the opening three games and Ryan showed resolution in getting off to her 2–1 lead. Then Lenglen's anticipation and the mesmerizing placement of her shots routed the challenger who, nonetheless, was to gain a permanent niche on the honor roll at Wimbledon by sharing nineteen doubles championships—twelve in women's of which six were with Lenglen, and the rest in mixed. Four decades later Billie Jean King came along to win or share in nineteen titles at the shrine but try as she might—and did—Billie Jean couldn't add the twentieth. At any rate, there was no question about Lenglen's supremacy over Ryan in singles; trailing 2–1, the French mademoiselle ran off eleven straight games for a 6–2, 6–0 victory.

There was now the increasing demand that Lenglen play in the United States. She had faced few American women in her climb to world eminence and, the U.S. being the U.S., no right-thinking American figured she was worth a quarter until she did something west of the Statue of Liberty. She had beaten Ryan, of course, and earlier in 1921 had eliminated the U.S. champion Molla Bjurstedt Mallory from the French hard-court championships. But otherwise all of her triumphs had been at the expense of Europeans.

For whatever reason—her fragile health, maybe— Lenglen had resisted a trip to America but she was drawn to U.S. soil in August 1921 by the suggestion she and Mallory play a series at the fashion spas along the eastern seaboard for charity, with proceeds to war-ravaged French towns. So she and her parents set off from Le Havre.

Asthma and seasickness took a toll in the crossing, and a heat wave and high humidity added to her discomfort upon her arrival in New York. The national championships were ready to begin at Forest Hills and she was persuaded by tournament officials and the press to delay the matches with Mallory and compete in them. She agreed reluctantly. She was drawn in the first round against Eleanor Goss, who promptly defaulted. That brought Lenglen against defending champion Molla in the unseeded draw.

Mallory had been getting ready for this for weeks. She launched a driving attack from the outset, so fierce that Lenglen gained only two games in the first set. Coughing and complaining of giddiness, she signalled her father in the gallery. He hurried to her side bearing a tiny flask of brandy. She sipped some, poured some on sugar cubes and sucked those returning to the baseline to undertake the second set, snakebite apparently belayed.

She served, waved feebly at Mallory's return, and double-faulted. Then she walked hesitantly to the umpire's chair. *"Je regret."* She said she was sorry to be too ill to continue. She packed her racquets and made her way to the locker room. The crowd was stunned and the hard-thinking newshounds ready to pounce. Next day's headlines charged her with quitting under fire.

She abandoned the charity series with Mallory, leaving war-torn French villages to their own resources, and set sail for home. Medical certificates attested to her illness but criticism was not foreshortened. For months in subsequent matches, whenever she complained of an onslaught of the vapors or vented her celebrated temperament, she was disparaged.

A year later, though, she returned to the familiar surroundings of Wimbledon. By then the challenge round concept had been dispensed with and seeding introduced to include the defending champion. Lenglen and Mallory won through to the final. The betting shops in Fleet Street placed the shorter price on the American.

Actually, Mallory was a native of Norway, the top women's player of the sardine capital for a decade before exposing herself to the wilds of Brooklyn in 1914 to visit her mother's cousin. She had scarcely unpacked her tennis racquet when she learned that the women's national indoor championships were coming up at the Seventh Regiment Armory. Her game was rusty but she entered anyhow. And being accustomed to indoor play helped her survive early rounds as she got the cobwebs out of her strokes. Surprisingly, when she met Marie Wagner in the final she was a shade better on her aggressiveness, and she edged out a 6–4, 6–4 verdict. That convinced Molla Bjurstedt that Norway was a nice place to visit but she'd rather live in Brooklyn.

Her game grew there too. She won the women's national championship four years in a row before Hazel Hotchkiss Wightman unseated her in 1919. Hazel might not have if Molla had not headed off for Palm Beach on a tennis excursion and met a New York stockbroker, Franklin I. Mallory, who took her mind off tennis. Six months later they were married. They settled in an apartment on Fifth Avenue, and hard-thinking sportswriters drew sighs of relief that they'd rarely be called upon to spell Bjurstedt again.

Picking up competitive tennis in 1920 Molla swept three more Forest Hills singles championships through 1922, yielded to Helen Wills for the next three years, then won her eighth national in 1926. She won two women's doubles crowns with Eleanora Sears, too, and two mixed with Bill Tilden.

And so Molla was in the midst of compiling this compelling record when she faced Lenglen on Wimbledon's impeccable lawns in 1922. It was not her day, as the August match at Forest Hills had not been Lenglen's.

Mallory made no excuses, though, even as Lenglen brought the full scope of her game to bear in a 6–2, 6–0 win.

A rubber match was arranged in Nice at Suzanne's home court but Mallory's concentration was divided. She and Franklin swept in the sights of the Riviera, even touring the casinos of Monte Carlo the night before the match. Suzanne, meantime, was at her most murderous and when the women took up their baseline positions the execution was quick—6–0, 6–0.

Suzanne was almost that invincible again in 1923 wherever she played, but in 1924 she was set back by jaundice and had to give up defense of her French championship. She went to Wimbledon in late June, however, and seemed thoroughly recovered as she achieved the unique feat of reaching the quarterfinals without losing a solitary game. There, she engaged her frequent rival and doubles partner Elizabeth Ryan. The match seemed no different from any other until the second set when Lenglen lost her control and then her touch. Ryan won the set easily and led 4–1 in the third. Yet she couldn't bring it off. Lenglen, pale and apparently playing under considerable distress, pulled out the match. Through it all, even when hardest pressed, Suzanne's attitude had remained flawless—no decision was questioned, there were no swoons, no histrionics, no petulant whimpers. But she was sent to bed by physicians and was unable to get approval from them to play her semifinal match. She defaulted and did not play again all year.

And then there was another of her all-conquering years in 1925. She swept the French and Wimbledon singles, teamed with Elizabeth Ryan and Jean Borotra to win the doubles and the mixed there, and with Didi Vlasto and Jacques Brugnon for the doubles titles in France.

No one in modern times went through Wimbledon winning as many love sets as the immortal mademoiselle did that summer. Nor has the holder of either the men's or women's singles title ever been beaten 6–0, 6–0 as was Kitty McKane, later Mrs. L. A. Godfree, in that year's semifinal. McKane had won the 1924 championship following Lenglen's default, and she was to win it again in 1926.

But in 1925 Suzanne's record in winning her sixth and last Wimbledon championship was phenomenal. She beat Ryan 6–2, 6–0, and put out Elsie Goldsack, a leading British player and later a Wimbledon semifinalist, by 6–1, 6–0. Winifred Beamish, a British Wightman Cup player, didn't win a game in the quarterfinal and Kitty McKane didn't in the semis, either. Lenglen demolished Britain's No. 2 player Joan Fry in the final by 6–2, 6–0 so that in the ten sets she played seven were won at love. In her headlong rush to the championship the volatile Frenchwoman dropped only five games. No succeeding champion has ever approached that record.

Obviously, Lenglen had run out of opponents. But wait. Across the sea a new star was emerging, young and stronger even than the formidable Molla Mallory. This was Helen Wills, an impassive young woman of twenty so stoical on court that the name Little Miss Poker Face became her sobriquet. By 1926 she had won the U.S. title three times in a row. There was, therefore, an inevitable and growing pressure wherever tennis was played for a match between them.

After long negotiation the players agreed to meet at the Carlton Tennis Club in Cannes in February 1926. Special grandstands were built but, even so, not nearly enough seats were available for the throng. Ticket price was set at $11, an enormous figure then. Still, interest was intense enough that when the match was undertaken scalpers were getting five times that amount.

It was, by all accounts, a marvellous match. Lenglen won it 6–3, 8–6. James Thurber was there for *The New Yorker* reporting that the underdog Californian "met for the first time the greatest woman tennis player in the world since the time when Helen was fondling dolls, [and she] fought her with everything she had, smashed with her, drove with her, volleyed with her, until she had the French champion so greatly on the run that at times it seemed like the baseline on Mlle. Lenglen's side of the court was the dropping-off place. It was a match that transcended statistics." It should not be forgotten in the wake of this panegyric that Wills lost.

So there was no disputing that Lenglen at twenty-seven was the supreme women's player. Promoters implored her to become a professional. She was tempted but she was even more anxious to match the Wimbledon record of seven singles championships owned by Dorothea Douglass Chambers. Chambers won there in 1903, 1904 and 1906 under her maiden name, Dorothea Douglass, and then added four championships as Mrs. Lambert Chambers in 1910, 1911, 1913 and 1914. Thus, after sweeping to another French championship—with, incredibly, the loss of only *four games*—Lenglen headed once more for Wimbledon. And, this time, to disaster.

There were politics in tennis, then as now. For whatever reasons, the French and the American associations resented the long-standing doubles partnership of Lenglen and Ryan, and they decreed that each must take a countrywoman as her partner in national tournaments. Both players were upset by the decision, which they regarded as spiteful. Though they had won six of the preceding seven women's doubles finals at Wimbledon, neither was dependent on the other for doubles success. Lenglen, for instance, had won the French twice in a row with Didi Vlasto and Ryan had won the American with Eleanor Goss.

Lenglen's fury was not abated either when she arrived at Wimbledon to find that she and Vlasto had to play Ryan and her new partner Mary K. Browne in the first match. On top of that, Lenglen was to play Browne, a rising youngster, in the first round of the singles. All in all, her diva's temperament was getting a strenuous workout for her first day in England. When Browne took five games from her in the singles match, the high-strung French star was ready to ax down the grandstand.

The doubles match was scheduled late on the afternoon following Lenglen's singles match with Browne. She made a doctor's appointment for early afternoon. Accounts of what followed are conflicting, but apparently Wimbledon officials were notified by an appointments secretary in Buckingham Palace that King George V and Queen Mary would be driving down to Wimbledon in their Rolls Royce next afternoon for the matches. With nothing of consequence scheduled, drawmakers hastily scheduled Lenglen's second-round match for the centre court at 2 o'clock. Apparently several officials felt someone else had advised the toast of Paris of this change in the day's lineup.

Checking with her partner next morning, Didi Vlasto happened to mention to Lenglen that she would not have much time between her singles and their doubles that afternoon. Lenglen, her nerves already taut and her patience with tennis officials on the shortest of fuses, was ready to set fire to her bed. She claimed later that she called *les cochons* at Wimbledon to tell them she couldn't possibly play two matches on such notice. She even called her sometime doubles partner, Jacques Brugnon, to tell him to tell *les vaches* at Wimbledon that she'd not be there for a 2 o'clock match. Whatever, word didn't get through.

At 1:45 the royal party arrived in an auto cavalcade, pennants waving from tiny staffs on the front fenders, and took their places under the cloth canopy behind the baseline. They had been advised by Wimbledon officials that none other than Suzanne Lenglen was playing at 2. To their dismay, nothing much transpired on the lawn before them except that workmen removed the net and the posts, baring the court which they then rolled and rerolled, impassive and leisurely.

At 3:30 who should arrive at Wimbledon but the world's finest women's tennis player. She was summoned by the tennis committee and sternly rebuked for keeping Their Majesties waiting. What did a poor little French girl care about a couple of English royals? Suzanne flew into a tantrum and then into the women's dressing quarters. She refused to emerge from either. Another of her doubles partners, Jean Borotra, tip-toed into the boudoir, fearful of both Suzanne and the fact no man had ever been known to darken the sanctified doorstep, even a Frenchman by dark of night. No matter. Herself was not to be placated. Borotra was dispatched by committeemen to the royal box to apologize on behalf of his countrywoman. The way the press played the incident, *la belle de France* had deliberately affronted the English monarchs. When she finally appeared, she and Vlasto were quickly eliminated by the Americans Ryan and Browne. Then Lenglen lost her singles match to unknown Mrs. J. G. Dewhurst of Ceylon. Lenglen stomped from the court, from London and from England, refusing to grant interviews.

Later that year she accepted a huge guarantee, said to be $50,000, from Charles C. (Cash and Carry) Pyle, a celebrated American promoter, to tour with, among others, Mary K. Browne and the brilliant Vincent Richards. But illness plagued her chronically and though her earnings from the successful tours made her remaining days comfortable financially, her health continued to deteriorate and she was dead before she reached forty.

How good was Suzanne Lenglen? It's impossible to compare players of different generations, of course, but if Bill Tilden can be rated the greatest ever in spite of the advances made in equipment and technique for stars such as Connors and Laver and Borg in the 1970s, then Lenglen must be held superior to King and Evert and Court, the three finest a half century after Suzanne reigned. Sometimes Helen Wills is regarded as the all-time best, but not in the book of a woman who played against Lenglen and Wills and partnered both of them.

This is Elizabeth Ryan, whose nineteen Wimbledon titles are unsurpassed. Once, long after the retirement of

Wills and Lenglen, she was encountered by the syndicated columnist for the Hearst papers and a widely read magazine sportswriter, Bob Considine. Who was the best, Bob wanted to know in 1941.

"Suzanne, of course," snapped Ryan without hesitation. "She owned every kind of shot, plus a genius for knowing how and when to use them. I worked with her quite a bit around the start of the war when she was fourteen or fifteen. In fact, I beat her in one of those early tournaments. But just after that she won the championship of France and she never was beaten thereafter. You realize what that means? She just never lost. She walked off the court after Molla Mallory won a set from her at Forest Hills but she could have beaten Molla any other day by almost any score she chose.

"She never gave an opponent the same kind of shot to hit twice in a row. She'd make you run miles. She wouldn't really sock more than two shots a set; her game was all placement and deception and steadiness. I had the best drop shot anybody ever had but she could not only get up to it but was so fast that often she could score a placement off of it. She had a stride a foot and a half longer than any known woman who ever ran, but all those crazy leaps she used to take were done after she hit the ball. Sure, she was a poser, a ham in the theatrical sense. She had been spoiled by tremendous adulation from the time she was a kid, but she was the greatest woman player of them all. Never doubt that."

*Helen Wills*

# HELEN WILLS

## [1905–    ]

Helen wills was never the kid next door.

Oh, in 1922 when first she went east from her native San Francisco to the national championships, a leggy youngster of sixteen, pink-cheeked and excited, wearing two long bouncing pigtails with bows in them, there was something of Mom's Apple Pie about her. But soon she became a champion and from then on she wore a stoic's facade, utterly emotionless on the tennis court, an icicle.

There is no question that she was the finest player of her day; the only question now is whether she was the best ever. It is another of those imponderables, impossible to settle. Almost anyone who has ever scowled at an umpire's call agrees that Wills and Suzanne Lenglen must be rated with Billie Jean King and Chris Evert at the top of the heap, but the order depends on whom you read.

The difference between Wills and Lenglen was the difference between power and finesse. Wills, like Lenglen, developed her natural talents through intensive practice. She became a powerhouse partly by modelling her forehand on that of the man who whipped Tilden in the 1919 national finals, William (Little Bill) Johnston. By the mid-1920s Wills was hitting the ball harder than most men, particularly off her forehand. She did not have the fi-

31

nesse, the swiftness of movement, the courtcraft or the ballerina's grace of Lenglen. She was graceful so long as she did not have to run. Her service was not remarkable, and her volleying no more than adequate. So she was not the player at doubles she was at singles, but she was by no means a Grecian urn either. She partnered four players in winning seven major doubles titles, four at Forest Hills and three at Wimbledon—Elizabeth Ryan, Hazel Hotchkiss Wightman, Mary K. Brown and Margaret Z. Jessup.

Nobody has a singles record to match hers—not the adored Lenglen, not the oft-crowned King, and not another notable ice maiden, Evert. Wills won the singles championship a record eight times at Wimbledon. She won seven national titles at Forest Hills and four French championships in Paris. During one stretch of five years from 1927 to 1932 she never lost a solitary set, much less a match, in competition, and six years after that, in 1938 when she was closing on thirty-three and fourteen years after her first appearance at Wimbledon, she won her final singles title there.

"Such was the assertive power of her trenchant drives on either wing, such was her freedom from error, and such was her cold unswerving determination that she crushed opposition like a machine," wrote Lance Tingay, the tennis correspondent for the London *Daily Telegraph*.

Wills became known internationally as Little Miss Poker Face, an appelation pinned on her first by W. O. McGeehan, New York sportswriter of an era remembered as the Golden Age of Sport, a period in which Wills and Tilden, Red Grange and Babe Ruth, Jack Dempsey and Bobby Jones won boundless encomiums in the press.

Wills also became known in America as Our Helen and Queen Helen. She was strikingly attractive in a remote and icy way, and historians note that the black-and-white photography of the day did no justice to her glowing complexion or smooth oval features. She had, one of them wrote, "the pervading serenity of sculptured marble." On the court she appeared as a robot designed to pound a tennis ball forever. "One could never imagine that the possibility of defeat existed in her mind," Lance Tingay noted, "but what thoughts and emotions lay within the chill splendor of her outward form were never revealed."

In a bland autobiography called *Fifteen–Thirty* published in 1937, Wills recounts that in early youth she adopted a white eyeshade as protection against the California glare. Once she succeeded Lenglen as the Wimbledon champion her eyeshade replaced Suzanne's bandeaux in every imaginable situation, even at fashionable bridge tables. The clothes designer Ted Tinling recalled once that when Wills first appeared at Wimbledon she wore her school uniform consisting of a white middy blouse with a black tie over a wide-pleated skirt. Playing with rare interruptions at Wimbledon for fourteen years from 1924 till 1938 she varied this costume only in such minor details as discarding the tie, arranging slight alterations in the shape of the collar and modifying her skirt lengths. "Another feature that seemed to have a permanent place in her wardrobe," Tinling related, "was a cerise-colored, lambs-wool cardigan."

Once she became a champion Wills hobnobbed with the socially elite and generally had nothing to do with her opponents off the court and as little as possible with the ink-stained wretches writing about her. Similarly, she could restrain her enthusiasm for the drooling throngs cordoned off by police at Forest Hills and Wimbledon. "She attracted admiring but not exactly warm audiences," Richard Schickel observes in *The World of Tennis,* "and though looking back from an age in which personality is everything one must admire her refusal to play to the galleries, one cannot say that she did a great deal to make women's tennis a colorful or very stirring affair."

But Gianni Clerici in his voluminous *Tennis* gurgles over the same research Schickel exposed himself to. He finds that the autobiography, for instance, "reveals a witty and enchanting woman . . . Whether she was having supper with George Bernard Shaw or with the Duke of Gloucester, whether she was sporting in the snow on the Jungfrau or in the sea near Stockholm, Helen was always disarmingly simple and sincere. . . . The legend of Helen's aloofness and of her indifference is perhaps the result of the needs of others who want a champion of great complexity and simplicity all rolled into one."

The novelist Paul Gallico was a contemporary of this woman whose poise and hauteur affected so many people. In 1938 Gallico brought out his classic *Farewell to Sport* upon his departure as a sports columnist from the New York *Daily News* to undertake fiction writing. He believed the press spoiled her—and most of the era's other gifted athletes—"making complete egoists out of normal young men and women by writing too much about them. Helen Wills, at first a shy, normally sweet young girl, did not become really difficult until after she had been a champion for a few years, developed into an unbeatable player, was sought after by the society-conscious tennis crowd, and had been presented at the court of St. James's. And by that time it was too late. She had already, on our sports pages and in our headlines, become Our Helen, America's own little girl."

As a youngster, Willis had no great urge to be a champion. Her family was well off, her father a doctor in Berkeley, California, where Helen was born on October 6, 1905. She started tennis because a little boy next door was always wanting to play it. When her autobiography was published in 1937 she noted that she always regarded tennis "as a diversion and not as a career."

At thirteen she travelled east to a boarding school in Vermont and didn't play tennis at all. A year later she took it up again; her father, returning from France where he'd served at a U.S. Army base hospital, bought her a junior membership at the Berkeley Tennis Club on her fourteenth birthday. She had a natural aptitude, was easily the best player among the junior girls and soon was playing the boys. It was really by accident that she discovered how well she could hit a ball, playing against one Frances Williams, who had been the best junior until she came along.

"It was while playing with Frances one afternoon that I first hit a real drive," she recalled. "I didn't know exactly how I had made the stroke, but I knew it was a drive and that I could do it again. We had been watching William Johnston in an exhibition match and were saying 'Now, I'm Johnston.' 'Watch me, I'm Johnston.' I had evidently learned something about the stroke from watching this great player in action."

After Frances moved away, Helen played the junior boys and when she overran her opposition there she played the men, though this was not her idea. "Had it not been for white-haired, jolly-faced Mr. William Fuller, whom the members called 'Pop' I might have pined for games and had no one to play with. He arranged matches for me with better players." Pop Fuller, who later helped develop another Californian, Helen Hull Jacobs, showed Wills how to play the game properly.

By sixteen she emerged as the best player on the West Coast. She won the Pacific Coast junior championship, the national eighteen-and-under title and was chosen to represent the state in the U.S. National Junior Championships at Forest Hills. There, she saw Suzanne Lenglen, who was making her first, and last, appearance in America.

"I was impressed when she came out to practice with six racquets," Wills remembered of the Belle of France. "Her sleeveless dress with its short fluttering pleated skirt was the first of its kind to be seen at Forest Hills. A gold bracelet flashed in the sun above the elbow on her left arm, and a bright-colored head-band held her short black hair neatly in place. A trim and dainty figure with especially slender ankles, and feet that twinkled when she ran, she made a pleasing picture for the dozen newspaper cameras gathered on the sidelines."

She watched the match that became a *cause célèbre* on two continents—Lenglen's default to the American champion Molla Mallory, an act that Helen herself was to duplicate years later when she played Helen Jacobs and defaulted while trailing. She claimed after the Jacobs match that the magnitude of her act really hadn't occurred to her, a curious observation in light of her awareness of the Lenglen controversy. "A discussion went from one end of the sporting world to the other," she wrote. "Even people who had never seen a tennis match in their lives were talking about it."

The following year in 1922 when Wills was not yet seventeen, she reached the Forest Hills women's singles final and was dismantled by Mallory winning her third straight U.S. championship and seventh in eight years. The match marked the beginning of Helen's trademark. Little Miss Poker Face took her whipping with not so much as a frown, and one year later she was back with the same expressionlessness, crushing Mallory and becoming at not-yet-eighteen the national champion with a ruthless 6-2, 6-1 dominance.

That was the year the Wightman Cup matches were launched, an annual transatlantic classic between U.S. and British women, five matches of singles and two of doubles. Helen was chosen on an American team that swept the Brits 7-0 (the next year Britain got even, 6-1).

By then, Wills's skills were drawing almost the attention of her impassive features. "She is powerful, repressed and imperturbable," wrote the dean, W. O. McGeehan, in the *Herald-Tribune*. "She plays her game with a silent deadly earnestness, concentrated on her work. That, of course, is the way to win games, but it does not please galleries."

Helen was not always as unemotional as her facade indicated, a fact revealed in her first visit to England and Wimbledon, which was anything but a triumph. What was overlooked in the ensuing mild furor was that the trip was her first away from the North American continent and that she was still only eighteen.

She lost both singles matches in the Wightman Cup as

the British came within one victory of matching America's sweep of the previous summer. Their only loss was to Wills and partner Hazel Hotchkiss Wightman, the founder of the international series, whose idea in it was to provide "a new and definite objective" for women along the lines of the Davis Cup for men.

Following the Wightman Cup matches Wills reached the final in her first Wimbledon tournament and engaged England's leading player, Kathleen McKane. It was also her first appearance before royalty. Queen Mary was seated at the end of the court under the mauve and green canopy, accompanied by the Duke and Duchess of York.

A straight-set victory seemed in the offing for Helen. She won the opener at 6–4 and sped to a 4–1 lead in the second. She netted two opportunities to increase the margin to 5–1, then didn't pursue a lob that looked out but fell just in and gave McKane the sixth game. Encouraged, the Briton lifted her pace, forced errors and, feeding on the growing enthusiasm of the capacity gallery, she completed a run of five games to win the set at 6–4 and level the match. At 3–3 in the decisive set McKane broke Helen with a net-cord shot and that did it. When each held service in the next three games, the British champion earned her Wimbledon crown on the 6–4 finale.

Helen, nonetheless, found the match filled with affirmatives. It gave her the feel of Wimbledon's hallowed centre court, and impressed upon her the necessity of complete concentration, especially late in the match. She began to repeat the simple phrase, "Every shot," as she played to remind herself to concentrate on each phase of her game, and to chase down shots, even those that appeared to be out. She also learned to seal her stoicism, for in this match she cracked a little, crying when McKane scored the final point. Tennis writers in London's national newspapers chided her, the ice queen, for weeping in defeat.

This was 1924, the year of the Paris Olympics, a time when tennis was part of the Games. Helen helped turn the matches into an American rout. She won the singles and partnered Molla Mallory to win the doubles. All that detracted from a shower of Olympic gold was that Suzanne Lenglen did not compete. There was by now a growing insistence on the continent she and Helen clash on court.

The opportunity did not materialize for another eighteen months. In January 1926 Wills left her studies at the University of California and with her mother went to the south of France where Lenglen was in demand along the Riviera. Indeed, she was idolized along that rich strip of the Mediterranean. John Tunis wrote once in *The New Yorker* that tourists could no more afford to miss Lenglen there than to go to Rome and not visit St. Peter's.

"If she does not play, there will be a vast void of empty seats," Tunis related. "When she omitted the Monte Carlo meeting it cost the *Societe des Baines de Mer,* who run the Casino and the tennis and the golf and the theatre and the opera and everything else at Monte, exactly 40,000 francs, a lot of money to lose in one week."

When Lenglen and Wills entered the annual tournament at the Carleton Club in Cannes, excitement was fanned along the coast. "Never has the Riviera been like this, at least in the six winters I have known it," Tunis

39

wrote. "Tennis and Suzanne, tennis and Helen Wills, that is the chief topic of conversation. People who until last week did not know whether tennis was a game or something to eat now discuss footwork and the difference in balls and climate with the greatest authority.

"Picture the scene when the two clash—the sunswept court, the green hills beyond in the distance, the blue Mediterranean stretching out to the horizon. And around the court the socially elite of Europe, the King and the Crown Prince of Sweden, the Duke of Westminster, who owns half of the city of London and is the richest peer in Great Britain, besides hundreds of other lesser nobility from all over the continent."

Among the scores of newspapermen arriving in Cannes was the celebrated Paris correspondent of the *Herald-Tribune,* Sparrow Robertson. "He confronted me with the question, 'Well, what have you got to say for yourself?' " Wills wrote later. "This surprised me more than any other of the hundreds of questions that I had to try to find some answer for in many interviews. I still clung, by now rather desperately, to the fundamental idea that I was on the Riviera to play tennis."

Eventually, that's what she did, advancing steadily through her half of the draw. So did the Maid Marvel of France in the other half. Inevitably, each gained the final. God knows what might have happened had they not—excitement had reached new highs as the end of the tournament neared, and scalpers were getting $50 a ticket by the time the final day dawned, a delightful one, the sky blue, the air fresh, the sunshine sparkling.

Reflecting on the match Wills quoted a prominent Spanish novelist, Vincente Blasco Ibanez, who had been engaged by a European press service to take his fiction-writer's eye to courtside. "I confess that I am a very incompetent judge of games," Ibanez said, "but then I know something about psychology and as a novelist am a trained observer so that I quickly realized I was watching a very tense contest. Mlle. Lenglen was high-strung and fidgety, Miss Wills cool and strong. . . . Mlle. Lenglen had the sympathy of the crowd. I personally feel that the day she plays before icy, indifferent, impartial spectators, she will lose most of her admirable qualities of play . . . but the cool, well-poised contender is always mistress of herself, and will always go to the front. In the end, Miss Wills will defeat Mlle. Lenglen, though not this day."

Helen's own reflection on the match, won by Lenglen at 6–3 and 8–6, was that though the French wizard didn't hit the ball hard, she was "uncannily steady" and hit "with a precision that seemed almost unbelievable." Lenglen's strategy was to keep Wills on the run and the ball in play, and Wills's was to rely on her superior endurance to wear down the Frenchwoman. In a sense, both followed the prescribed plan except that Lenglen didn't wear down quite soon enough for Wills to administer a coup de grace, though she seemed headed in that direction in the elongated second set, leading 5–4 and 40–30. She laced a drive down the line on Lenglen's forehand that seemed to be the set-winner. But the ball was a trifle long.

Interestingly, Lenglen had to make a major psychological adjustment to pull off the clinching game, a feat for her when it's remembered that the principal criticism of her game was that she tended to fall apart when outside forces weren't slanted her way.

Leading 6–5 and holding match point, she couldn't get

to a Wills forehand. But the cry of "out!" gave her the point, apparently, and with it the match. The players shook hands at the net and photographers were snapping pictures as the women turned to thank the chaired umpire when linesmen hurriedly commanded his attention. The umpire, Commander Hillyard, who was Wimbledon's centre court umpire, leaned forward to hear them. The baseline linesman, Lord Charles Hope, said he had not made the out call nor had the sideline official, Cyril Tolley. It had been the cry of someone in the crowd. So the score was deuce instead of game. In the resumption of play Wills won that game, sending the score to 6–6, and this was assuredly as good a time as any for the volatile Lenglen to fold. Instead, she won two games in a row. Only then did she pause to reveal the full flower of her French temperament by sitting down and weeping, cuddling a bouquet of American Beauty roses.

Wills was soon joined by a young San Francisco stockbroker Frederick Shander Moody, Jr., whom she'd met at Cannes and who was courting her. (Indeed, they were married three years later in 1929, then divorced ten years after that. In 1941 Helen married a California polo player and racing steward, Aidan Roark.) In any event, when young Moody lent his support following the Lenglen match she took a moment to reflect on the French star's game. She discovered then that she was surprised how much better Lenglen *played* then she *appeared* to play. In her memoirs she expanded on this appraisal: "Her control and delicacy of placement will probably never be equalled. In comparing other players to her I find none in the same class."

It was the only time the two world-ranking players were to meet across the net. Later that spring Wills was removed from the tennis scene by appendix surgery and Lenglen moved to professional ranks.

But Wills, really, was just getting her career nicely underway in spite of her precocious beginning. She was twenty the February she played Lenglen; the surgery kept her out of Wimbledon so that she didn't win the first of her eight singles titles there until the following summer, 1927. Surgery also kept her out of the U.S. nationals, breaking a string of championships she'd started at Forest Hills in 1923 and was to resume in 1927 for another three years. Thus she accounted for six titles there in the seven-year span, and her seventh came in 1931.

There was far more in the life of Helen Wills than tennis, almost all of it at a social level vastly different from most people's. For instance, she was presented at Buckingham Palace to Queen Mary, to the Prince of Wales who became Edward VIII, and to his brother Prince George who when Edward abdicated became George VI. "We enjoyed the delicious cold supper and sipped champagne served from golden coolers," she remembered. "Everyone was standing, balancing plates and glasses. And the swords of the officers in full dress were dangerous."

She sketched tennis players at Wimbledon and when Frank Crowninshield of the magazine *Vanity Fair* learned of and saw them he bought five for a full page in his magazine. One day at the home of Julian Myricks, the president of the USLTA, she met Ring Lardner at tea.

She asked him to sign her autograph book. The humorist dashed off a poem:

> *It surely does delight-us,*
> *That you've beat appendicitus.*

While recovering from her operation she painted at home in California in a studio her father had had built in the garden. She did a series of fashion drawings for B. Altman and Company, a New York department store, drew sketches for the White Star Steamship Company, and did half a dozen designs for a silk company. In London she went to lunch at Lady Astor's on St. James's Square and was seated across from George Bernard Shaw. ("His eyes were a marvellous blue, and as he was facing the light I could observe the changes of expression on his face, and the delightful twinkle that came and went in his eyes. His white hair and beard formed a mist about his ruddy face.") At various times she visited museums in New York, London, Berlin and Amsterdam with Dr. Wilhelm Valentiner, the world's first authority on Rembrandt. And there was a weekend at Cliveden, the country home of Lady Astor on the Thames. G.B.S. was there this time, too, and a few days afterwards sent her a copy of his *Saint Joan* with an inscription:

Dear Helen Wills:
I promised you this at Cliveden. You may remember stealing my heart on that occasion.

G. Bernard Shaw

19th July 1929

44

The British diplomat Viscount Lord d'Abernon introduced her to the painter Augustus John who did her portrait in oils and inscribed it "To Helen Wills in affectionate homage" over his signature, and in New York the Grand Central Art Galleries staged an exhibition of her drawings and sketches. Frank Crowninshield, the editor, wrote a foreword for the show's catalogue which said in part: "For her models she has selected the figures she knows best—the ranking tennis players of three continents. What is especially noticeable in her portrayals of them is her ability to convey the sensation of an authentic and continuing motion; she has added a feeling for contour and structural form that promises more important adventures in portraiture and painting."

Meantime, she was knocking off tennis championships in all directions. One year she shattered Molla Mallory in the U.S. nationals final by 6–0, 6–0. "Through it all the emotionless Helen Wills, her features an absolute mask of serene austerity, with never the flicker of a smile to lighten them, cut her older opponent down without even a pretense of mercy," marvelled Fred Hawthorne in the *Herald-Tribune.* "It was almost as though a man with a rapier were sending home his vital thrusts against a foeman unarmed."

Of all her championship matches, none was so controversial as the one at Forest Hills in 1933 and none more remarkable than her final appearance at Wimbledon in 1938. In the first she met the other Helen, Jacobs, her countrywoman and also a former pupil of her San Francisco coach Pop Fuller. In 1932 Wills had passed up the nationals and Jacobs had won her first championship there. In 1933 the two Helens reached the final. To the surprise of a capacity crowd in the horseshoe bowl Jacobs won the first set at 8–6, only the third time, astonishingly, that Wills had dropped a *set* in six years.

She came back at 6–3 in the second to ease the minds of the thousands who'd had an inkling an upset was brewing, but then the rising anticipation returned in the third set when Jacobs broke Queen Helen's serve, won her own, and broke the queen's again for a 3–0 lead. It appeared at long last and for the first time that the commoner was about to uproot the monarch.

But it wasn't to be. Trailing love-three, Wills made her way to the umpire's chair. "I can't go on," she said. She left the court.

In the ensuing furor there were few kind words for Our Helen. She was labeled a quitter and accused of depriving her opponent of a deserved moment in the sun. The public knew Wills had injured her back a few months earlier (the injury had received press attention) and that in her pain she had passed up the Wightman Cup matches that summer. Newspapers had published a letter from the chief surgeon at the New York Orthopedic Hospital, Dr. Benjamin Farrell, attesting to "a subacute unstable fifth lumbar vertebra symptom" in Wills's back. Still, no one wanted excuses; everyone wanted the queen's head at the foot of the guillotine.

In retrospect, Wills regretted that her injury had deprived Jacobs of complete victory, that her decision to withdraw had caused so violent a storm. "But being naturally selfish I thought only of myself," she said in her memoirs. "I could understand her feeling of disappoint-

46

ment, but the match would have ended in this way no matter against whom I had been playing."

The injury kept Wills out of competition in 1934. She swam and walked and underwent treatment for the sacroiliac condition, and returned to Wimbledon for renewed competition in 1935, not quite thirty and wondering if her skills had been permanently dulled. Again meeting Helen Jacobs on centre stage, she handled her by 6–3, 3–6 and 7–5, and with the winning threw aside her impassive facade for the first time since she'd cried in her maiden appearance at the tennis shrine. She squealed, hurled her racquet in the air and, laughing as she ran to the net, flung an arm across the weary shoulders of her opponent.

She considered retiring then. She had been a championship performer for thirteen years and, of course, in looking around could find no one left to beat. So she didn't lift a competitive racquet again until 1938. Then abruptly, hearing distant drums, she decided that she'd give the Wimbledon lawns she loved one more visit. She swept through the early rounds, gained the final, and in it she was opposed by her old rival and most persistent one, Helen Jacobs. Poor Helen Jacobs. In the ensuing hour it was as it had almost always been: too much other Helen. The queen had returned from her self-imposed exile. She swept to yet another championship, this time in straight sets and the second one at love.

But that *was* it. She never returned to play at Wimbledon or at Forest Hills or even at nearby Los Angeles Tennis Club. She settled into a private married life in Santa Monica in which tennis had almost no part. There were no more tournaments, no more headlines. She called the game "an exceedingly delightful dream which lasted for fifteen years." And after that it all became part of history.

# HELEN JACOBS

## [1908–    ]

*P*OOR HELEN JACOBS.

Wherever tennis players gathered all through the 1930s, it's doubtful if any other phrase found its way into the language with the regularity of that one.

Poor Helen Jacobs.

Anywhere tennis fans got together, everybody knew its significance. There was no need to say anything else, to expand or to clarify.

At first glance, it seems an unlikely adjective. Here was an attractive player who won the U.S. national singles title four times in succession, still a record, and who triumphed once at Wimbledon too. Still, it's an applicable adjective, all right, assuredly accurate in its spirit if not precisely in its letter.

For this was a champion who was more often a bridesmaid than a bride, the world's great runner-up who spent a career, it seemed, being crushed by Helen Wills. She was a finalist sixteen times in world-class events, and was beaten in eleven. Six times a finalist at Wimbledon and once a winner; twice a finalist in the French championships and never a winner; eight times a finalist at Forest Hills and four times sent reeling.

Most of the time it was Wills who pulled out the rug

*Helen Jacobs*

but, more significantly, Wills was in the lists only once when Jacobs won her five major titles—on the celebrated occasion when Queen Helen defaulted with Jacobs at long last on the brink of beating her. One other time in something like fifteen matches Jacobs held a match point on her tormentor—and she blew it. That was at Wimbledon in 1935. At a searing low point, Wills lashed her 6–0, 6–0 in a final at Seabright.

Jacobs never uttered a word publicly to put down her longtime rival and steadfastly refused to become involved in the controversy when newspapers insisted over and over that the women could scarcely stand the sight of one another. *There Was Never a Feud* was the title of a magazine piece under Jacobs's name. "During all the years in which we both were playing, we never once exchanged an unpleasant word!" Helen said, employing the exclamation mark. But Bill Tilden, a close friend of the younger Helen's, once wrote that she seethed in the wake of at least one match with Wills. "You know, Bill, I don't mind her being a so-and-so," Tilden says Jacobs told him, "but I object to her being a stupid so-and-so. If she had only smiled when she shook hands at the end and said, 'I'm glad you broke your damn leg'—or something like that."

This was the last time the two Helens played each other, this 1938 final at Wimbledon, and though soundly beaten, 6–4 and 6–0, Jacobs emerged with the tallest of psychological triumphs. In her quarterfinal match she had picked up a severe ankle injury, a tear in the sheath of the Achilles tendon. It was strapped for her semifinal match—against Alice Marble, another nemesis—as she advanced to her fifth Wimbledon final with Wills and fifth defeat.

It began as a tightly waged match, following service to 4–4. Jacobs was serving with a 40–30 lead in the ninth game when she leaped for a shot and landed heavily on one foot, jarring the already injured tendon. The ankle swelled. She was unable to run. She refused, however, to default even on the urging of Hazel Hotchkiss Wightman, donor of the trophy that bears her married name and a close friend and advisor of most of the American internationalists. She scarcely did more than go through the motions in the ensuing eight games, losing them all to the stoic across the net grinding them out like sausages.

Both players spoke silent volumes in closing the affair in this manner. Jacobs was saying, "Look, pal, this is how you finish a match when you're injured. You don't default, see?" And Wills was playing out her implaccable fifteen-year role. "My job's to hit the ball over the net," she was saying. "If you're hurt, don't play."

Throughout her career Jacobs was all heart and determination. Or, as Alice Marble phrased it, "She had more will to win, more drive and guts than anyone else." Her equipment was scanty by world standards. She had a forehand that never became much more than a defensive shot, and she was not a skilled volleyer. "I always thought she got the furthest with the leastest," George Lott, the Davis Cup doubles player, said once. "To be exact, she had a forehand chop, a sound backhand, and lots and lots of stomach muscles." By contrast Wills was a howitzer. Still, while she may not have ranked with Lenglen and Wills or Evert and King in the relative sense, hardly any experienced observer omits the name of Helen Jacobs from a list of the top ten women of all time. And there was no question the galleries preferred this game competitor to the impassive Helen, particularly since everyone was convinced, in spite of the denials of both players, that they had little love for one another. Jacobs summed up their relationship once by saying that to play against Wills was to play against a machine. "There was little, if any, conversation, no joviality, and to this the gallery obviously reacted, becoming almost grim in its partisanship," the other Helen noted. "The press people have long since confused incompatability with the elements of a feud in our matches which became less agreeable to both of us as they inevitably occurred. I remember no laughter from the crowded stands, though admiring applause was often thunderous. Helen Wills fought on court as much as Gene Tunney fought in the ring—with implaccable concentration and undeniable skill but without the color or imagination of a Dempsey or a Lenglen."

Jacobs and Wills had similar backgrounds though the popular notion that they were born in the same San Francisco neighborhood is inaccurate. They weren't even from the same state though both attended the University of California and both played at the Berkeley Tennis Club and shared the teaching ability of William (Pop) Fuller there. Almost three years separated them. Wills was born in October 1905 and Jacobs two years and ten months later in August 1908.

Jacobs was not a Californian. She was born in a whistle stop called Globe, in Arizona, where her father Roland worked with his brother-in-law, Frederick Alsdorf, a mining engineer who struck it rich with discovery of a copper mine in the mountains near Globe. Alsdorf and Jacobs married sisters named Hull. Hull became Helen's middle name.

The mine was fruitful for Alsdorf and Jacobs and their partners for half a dozen years (at one time the stock, originally $5 a share, was selling for $54 on the New York Curb Exchange) but then the ore began to peter out. The two families moved to San Francisco where Roland Jacobs settled into an executive's chair in the San Francisco *Chronicle*'s advertising department.

The climate aggravated a respiratory illness and Roland Jacobs was advised to exercise to help relieve it. He had a couple of tennis racquets and turned to the game, walking to courts at Lafayette Square and teaching his daughter the rudiments. In time her game developed enough so that she could handle Roland's best efforts. She entered a public courts tournament, won it, but still was not much interested. Indeed, writing was her main interest and for exercise she preferred swimming.

But the year Helen was fifteen San Francisco was suddenly thrilled that one of its own had won the national women's singles championship. This was Helen Wills, of course, whose success stirred yearnings in young Helen Jacobs to "go East," as the phrase went for anyone moving to New York. So she returned to tennis with new vigor, and a natural aptitude, a good eye and quick reflexes soon had her playing better than anyone of her age. One person her game impressed was Pop Fuller.

In Jacobs's autobiography *Beyond the Game,* and in the memoirs of Helen Wills, *Fifteen–Thirty,* the women gave tall credit to Fuller for developing their games. Maybe so. But in retrospect there are grounds to suspect Fuller may have inculcated a lifelong fear of Wills by Jacobs in that year of 1923 when, for whatever reason, he arranged a match between the two young women—the one on the brink of the national championship, the other hardly aware of the difference between a volley and a smash.

Jacobs didn't say so in her book but it's a hard thought to miss. "My tennis opponents up to this time knew no more about the game than I did," she wrote in 1936. "None was interested so much in study of the game as in victory with whatever strokes it could be achieved. For a week I looked forward to the game Mr. Fuller succeeded in arranging, and when the day arrived when I was to practice with Helen Wills I left school early and crossed the bay to Berkeley with my mother.

"I walked onto the court to meet Helen Wills for the first time. She looked very solemn and efficient in her white visor. As we commenced to rally I realized for the first time what speed of shot meant. The ball came straight as a die and fast as a bullet. In seven minutes from the time we started our game, she had beaten me 6–0."

Next morning Fuller telephoned to invite the Jacobs family to visit the Berkeley Tennis Club. There, they were introduced by Fuller to Dr. Clarence Wills and his wife, Helen's parents. Dr. Wills said he and his family were moving from their Berkeley home. He suggested that Jacobs take it so Helen could join the tennis club and eliminate the two-hour streetcar and boat ride from San Francisco. Roland Jacobs agreed, and from then on Helen's life became a daily routine of school and tennis.

Her opponents were usually men, and in training sessions Fuller threw balls for her to smash, volley or hit from either side. He carried the balls in a large box, eight dozen of them, and often he'd empty the box ten times in a session—960 throws. He taught Helen the proper way to hit each stroke, but she became more proficient with the backhand than any other. "It is the only part of my technical equipment that has never failed me," she wrote in 1936, still a world-ranking player.

On the day after her sixteenth birthday she was able to "go East" for the first time—the California association sent her to Philadelphia for the national junior championships. The nature of the times is reflected in the fact that the association—hopeful of making the journey rewarding for Helen and her mother—sent them to Philadelphia via Canada: nine days of train travel taking them north to Victoria on Vancouver Island, then east through the Rockies, across the Canadian prairies, through the national capital, Ottawa, and on into Montreal and Quebec City in the predominantly French-speaking province of Quebec, and then south to Boston, a city in the New England state of Massachusetts.

Hazel Hotchkiss Wightman put them up as house guests in Brookline, a Boston suburb, where Helen met Bill Tilden, the greatest player of his time, who later contributed to her swift improvement.

That autumn Wightman took her guests to watch the national men's final at Forest Hills where Tilden engaged the Californian Little Bill Johnston and tore him to shreds. In her memoirs a dozen years later, Jacobs noted that ink-stained second-guessers were hinting in 1936 that Tilden was overrated, that the Briton Fred Perry, then the Wimbledon and Forest Hills champion, could handle him, and that Ellsworth Vines and Henri Cochet likely could too. But Helen disagreed.

"If memory has not betrayed me, Tilden could have defeated any one of these without the loss of more than a set," she wrote.

Reflecting on that 1924 event, she remembered being impressed by Johnston's skills in handling the Australian champion Gerald Patterson in a semifinal match. Then, in turn, being amazed by the magic of Tilden toying with Little Bill in the final, 6–1, 9–7, 6–2. "There had not been a break in Tilden's brilliance, control or speed. One was conscious of the ball as an agent of his will. I have never seen such tennis since, and I don't believe I ever shall."

Tilden was a lordly and imperious man, some historians claim, but Jacobs was fascinated by him. He liked her too, though there was no romantic attraction between them. Tilden was thirty-one when she watched him play Johnston, and she was sixteen.

A year later he drew her aside one afternoon in the dining room of the Vanderbilt Hotel in New York to tell her what was wrong with her forehand. The best way to explain it was to demonstrate it, so they drove to Forest Hills, and while a friend of Helen's mother tossed tennis balls at the eager young player Tilden taught her the fundamentals of the undercut forehand, a chop that put bottom-spin on the ball and made the stroke a good defensive weapon. He literally kicked her feet into the proper position to deliver a forehand and occasionally took her racquet to demonstrate his points. A man variously described as haughty, arrogant and impatient,

Tilden spent two hours in a blistering sun to show Jacobs how to protect the forehand side, a weakness that would likely have proved her permanent undoing had he not interceded. The shot remained Helen's Achilles heel, but only under the severest pressure and only by the best of players.

Tilden's advice made Jacobs much too good for her peers. She won two United States junior championships, the second a runaway at 6–0 and 6–0, and while still eighteen was invited to try for the Wightman Cup team. The committee felt her showing in the eastern grass court events at the Essex club in Manchester, Massachusetts, and at Seabright and East Hampton might well establish her readiness for international competition.

She encountered America's No. 2 player Molla Mallory at Essex. Anxious to qualify to play against the British, she undertook the Mallory meeting with intensity. Mallory played with much less, her place on the team assured. Nonetheless, Mallory had no desire to be wiped out, a destination that seemed in store as the grim youngster won the first set at 6–0 and sped off to a 3–0 lead in the second.

At that point, Mallory beckoned her opponent to join her at the umpire's chair and presented a bizarre request. She had forgotten a diamond brooch, she said, a good-luck pin, and she'd appreciate it if the match could be delayed while she sent a friend for it. At eighteen, Jacobs felt she could hardly deny the No. 2 player in the country, and so when the umpire gave voice to no objection the friend was dispatched.

The delay gave Jacobs too much time to think. So close

to a smashing victory, she became tentative and cautious when the pin had been fetched and the match resumed, and Mallory ran off five games in short order.

But then Helen began lacing backhand drives down the lines again, drilling serves, and keeping the ball deep and in the corners with her new Tilden forehand. She tied the set, battled on even terms as the score climbed to 9–8 in her favor, and when she broke Mallory's service in the eighteenth game, she had won, 6–0, 10–8, and earned a place on America's team.

And Jacobs stayed there for the next dozen years—until the Wightman matches were interrupted by World War II. In 1927 she met Helen Wills in the U.S. final for the first time, and was beaten 6–0, 6–2. They met a year later, and Wills had no trouble then either, winning at 6–2 and 6–1. In 1929 at Wimbledon the result was precisely as decisive, 6–1, 6–2, and in 1931 Wills scored her most crushing victory of all, beating Jocobs in love sets in the final at Seabright. They were at it again in the Wimbledon final of 1932 when scores were 6–3, 6–1. Poor Helen.

Still, not everything was so bleak. During a mixed doubles match at Wimbledon in 1931 Jacobs dared to be different. She ventured onto centre court *without stockings,* a revolutionary departure that some thought might turn the cream sour in the strawberries-and-Devonshire cream. Wearing only ankle socks, Helen was embarrassed to the point of rushing to the dressing-room when Queen Mary unexpectedly arrived in the royal box back of the court. As the large gallery stood and faced Her Majesty while she was seated, a blushing Jacobs quickly pulled stockings over her limbs, thank God, and returned to the court.

Later, this practically shameless person had a pair of knee-length shorts tailored prior to the Forest Hills championships in 1933, recalling in her memoirs that she anguished for two weeks before deciding they were modest enough for public observation. "As luck would have it, we were scheduled to play on the far side of the stadium. I have never had a more nerve-wracking walk than I did from the marquee to court number two that afternoon. But as I took the balls from the ballboy and went to my side of the court several spectators facing me smiled encouragement and applauded. It was like an avalanche of approval to my shaking confidence."

And in her encounters with Helen Wills, a delicious moment seemed at last to have sought her out in 1933. She and Wills survived two thrilling semifinal matches at Forest Hills to earn final berths, Jacobs handling the tenacious Dorothy Round, the best of the British players, 6–4, 5–7, 6–2, and Wills getting past another excellent Brit, Betty Nuthall, after dropping the opening set 6–2. She won the next pair at 3 and 2.

Jacobs believed that at long last she had found a way to beat Wills, short of sighting her along the barrel of a high-powered rifle. In the French championships the nonpareil herself, Suzanne Lenglen, told Jacobs the way to do it was to force Wills to move for short cross-court shots and offered to rally with her to illustrate.

"We rallied endlessly," Jacobs recalled. "Lenglen was incredibly accurate. She would drive down the line, deep or short, to teach me to hit the cross-court shot from any spot between the baseline and the service line. This, combined with going to the net at every opportunity, gave me the edge in our famous singles final of 1933 at Forest Hills."

Allison Danzig of the *New York Times,* who devoted a good portion of a lifetime to his reports from the courts, believed Wills was below form in the first two sets of the contentious final. He believed equally that he'd never seen Jacobs play better—"fighting with the heart of a champion." Her undercut forehand had carried the match in her semifinal meeting with Dorothy Round, he wrote, and against Wills "it was remarkable for its uniform length and accuracy." She had other attributes too. "Her service was a big help, pulling her out of the hole repeatedly in the bitterly fought first set, and her volleying and overhead smashing were the most vivid seen in the tournament."

Since Jacobs was not renowned for either the volley or the smash, it is apparent she was enjoying a rare day. She won the first set 8–6, then dropped the second 6–3 as Wills abandoned her usual tactic of keeping the ball deep and resorted to drop shots, alternately playing the ball short and deep, keeping Jacobs on the run, up and back, up and back, running out the set from 3–3.

But that was her last strong assault. Serving to start the final set Wills uncharacteristically double-faulted twice. Jacobs took the game, held her own service, and attacked Wills in the third. The latter made two attempts to move in on the net but Jacobs passed her easily and went ahead 3–0.

Later, Jacobs recalled her impressions of the ensuing

moments: "I turned to the ballboy to receive the balls, but he was looking beyond me.

" 'May I have the balls, please,' I asked.

"He pointed toward the other end of the court. Helen was walking toward the umpire's chair and had begun to put on her sweater. I walked toward her and asked if anything was wrong.

" 'My leg is hurting,' she replied. 'I can't go on.'

" 'Would you like to rest for a minute?' I asked.

" 'No,' she replied, 'I can't go on.'

"That sums up our entire conversation, although one reporter quoted me as begging her to continue. I was later asked whether I thought Helen should have defaulted. In my opinion, only the player himself knows if he can go on, and who can presume to say that an opponent is or is not in great physical pain?"

It's a fact that Jacobs was deprived of the full victory flavor but she emerged from the match anointed while Wills was pilloried for not giving her long-suffering rival a complete triumph.

The default represented the second U.S. crown in a row for Jacobs and in the next two years she made it four by handling Sarah Palfrey by identical 6–1, 6–4 scores. Wills was absent both times.

Jacobs was showing up regularly in the Wimbledon final as well. She had lost to Wills in 1932, then was shaded two years later in a three-set struggle by Dorothy Round, a pleasant and pious Sunday School teacher. In 1935 she was across the net once more from Wills, another meeting that endured, almost as well remembered in ensuing decades as the default match of 1933. This one capped a return to competition by Wills who had rested and undergone osteopathic treatment for eighteen months following the Forest Hills debacle. She had occupied herself in the 1934 Wimbledon reporting for the *London Daily Mail,* and did not get back on the courts for another six months, at home in San Francisco in January 1935. Now here she was in the Wimbledon final. But this time Jacobs was convinced she would win an untainted victory over the wonderful Wills.

Wills hit strongly as ever from the baseline in the first set, and quickly ran up a 3–0 lead. Jacobs rallied, came within a point of moving ahead 4–3, but faded instead and lost the set at 6–3. She reversed that 6–3 margin in the second. In the third she played with palpable determination and got a 5–2 lead, and now at last she was on the brink of a victory without strings.

Again Wills rose to the challenge as Jacobs served for the set and the match, holding her off and climbing to 5–3. Jacobs was implaccable, though, and got match point as Wills served at 30–40. She seemed to have it too, pushing Wills deep and rushing in as Wills lifted a desperate lob well short.

"The ball dropped quicker than I anticipated," Jacobs wrote, "and caught me in an awkward position where I could neither smash nor volley. By the time I was ready to hit the overhead, the wind was carrying the ball down and I was practically on my knees." Her shot hit the tape at the top of the net and fell back, deucing the game. Reprieved, Wills won the next two points to climb to 5–4, then ran out the next three games. She'd done it again to poor Helen.

Remarkably, it required more than this heartbreaker to keep Jacobs down. She sailed for home and won her fourth consecutive national women's championship at Forest Hills in September. Obviously, if she could not be established as the world's best women's player she could not be dislodged as the world's second-best and, as such, she was offered a $50,000 guarantee to turn professional and tour against Wills. Both women rejected the bids, Jacobs on the grounds she had never won Wimbledon and was determined to do so. Accordingly, she was back there the following June.

By then, she had been a finalist four times in seven years and had lost all four, three to Wills and one to Dorothy Round. And again on this occasion, she swept through to the final, her fifth, and this time, engaging the European star Hilda Krahwinkel Sperling, she was once more involved in a cliffhanger, underlining the fact that Helen never did do anything simply that could be accomplished in some anguish.

She and Sperling divided the first two sets, and both played with great deliberation in the third, neither displaying a clear advantage until 5–5. Then, as Jacobs so often had done, she reached into her well of determination and broke Sperling to gain the lead for the first time in that last set. When she held service she had at long last earned her doggedly pursued Wimbledon crown.

She returned to Forest Hills looking for a fifth successive singles title, and was thwarted by a blonde, slim and youthful power-hitter, Alice Marble. Then she returned to Wimbledon to defend *that* prize and was thwarted again. She gained the final, all right, but this was the moment of a last hurrah by Helen Wills, the one in which Little Miss Poker Face ran out the second set unblinkingly when Jacobs refused to default upon reinjuring her damaged ankle.

In her concluding championship appearances, in 1939 and 1940, she won a place in the Forest Hills finals for the seventh and eighth times. She lost both to a new nemesis, Alice Marble.

*Alice Marble*

# ALICE MARBLE

## [1913–    ]

W HEN ALICE MARBLE was in full flight on a tennis court, there was no one more exhilarating. Men players heavily engrossed in tournaments hardly ever turned to watch women playing, but when Alice Marble was one of the women they poured from practice courts and locker rooms and bridge games to appreciate her style and verve.

"She played without restraint," Julius Heldman, the eminent tennis analyst, wrote once, "running wide-legged, stretching full out for the wide shots, and walloping serves and overheads. Her appearance was trim, her manner brisk, and her style exciting. She managed to play like a man and still maintain her feminine appeal."

She had that, all right, nicely proportioned at five-feet seven and in the area of a hundred and forty pounds, blonde and tanned from long training sessions at Palm Springs and Los Angeles. She combined a white jockey-cap with the first crew-neck T-shirts and she shortened her skirts to about six inches above the knee. Her flashing game was the first among women to rely upon the serve-and-volley technique, she was one of the first women to follow her forehand to the net at every opportunity, and her big serve was probably the best ever among women until Virginia Wade came along with hers. Her second serve was almost as lethal, a whopping jumper of an American twist.

"In doubles she was a delight," Heldman remembered. "She had a knack of poaching for the kill and she ate up the other man's speed. She was a killer volleyer. She played close to the net and she went for short sharp angles. She was as good a doubles partner as any but the very top men. She did have a great eye and fast reflexes, and she never lost the tomboy attitude at the net."

Marble was on the amateur scene for a relative fleeting moment but she made a lasting imprint. In the five seasons from 1936 through 1940 she won eighteen championships at Wimbledon and Forest Hills. An illness that persuaded two eminent physicians in Paris and New York that her tennis-playing days were over just as she was beginning to emerge as an internationalist at age twenty prevented her from acquiring tall honors earlier than 1936, and the outbreak of World War II plus the fact she turned professional in 1941 kept her from adding to that towering total.

Marble was the first champion of the twentieth century who did not become involved in a traumatic struggle with some eminent rival. Suzanne Lenglen was as temperamental as a diva at La Scala and underwent an attack of the vapours, at the very least, whenever Molla Mallory threatened her. Helen Wills turned all wishy-washy when Helen Jacobs was about to prove her mortal, and Jacobs was always running into a crushing setback whenever she seemed about to emerge from the pack. But Marble? Well, all Marble did was dust the chalklines with anybody harboring intentions of defeating her. In the groove, Alice was a hunk of marble.

She was most in the goove in 1939 when she won everything—three championships at Wimbledon, three at Forest Hills, and another three in Wightman Cup play— nine for nine. And she required only nineteen sets to win those nine, one above the minimum. She was wonderful at Wimbledon. She beat Germany's Hilda Sperling 6–0, 6–0 in the singles semifinals and Britain's Kay Stammers 6–2, 6–0 in the final. She and Sarah Palfrey won the women's doubles in straight sets, and she and Bobby Riggs won the mixed in straight sets.

Moving to Forest Hills that September, she whistled through to the singles final where Helen Jacobs wrenched a set from her, a 10–8 squeaker sandwiched between Marble's 6–0 and 6–4 wins. She combined with Australian Harry Hopman to win the mixed, and with her friend Sarah Palfrey the women's. And in the Wightman Cup she beat England's Mary Hardwick and Kay Stammers, and she and Palfrey swept their doubles.

In 1940 there was no Wimbledon, the war with Germany having been undertaken by the British the previous September, but while the United States stayed out and the nationals graced the lawns at Forest Hills as usual, Marble won her third straight singles title, beating Jacobs in straight sets, defended the women's doubles with Palfrey for their fourth win in a row, and partnered Riggs in winning the mixed. In all, the blonde young woman from California won four mixed doubles titles at Forest Hills with four different partners: Gene Mako, Don Budge, Hopman and Riggs. As Julius Heldman had said, "She was as good a doubles partner as any but the very top men."

After wiping out everything and everyone in 1939 and most peacetime courts in 1940, there was nothing left for Marble to aspire to. She turned professional late in 1940 and toured with Mary Hardwick, Budge and Bill Tilden. A few years later she suffered a recurrence of her illness. A lung was removed, ending her competitive days but hardly slowing her social enjoyment of the game, and when she was in her mid-forties in 1959 she began giving lessons on weekends to the emerging Billie Jean King, then a tomboy young woman of sixteen wearing her family name, Moffitt. Years later, King recalled that what she'd gotten most from four months of work with Marble was a sense of what it was to be a champion.

"She talked a lot about Budge and Riggs, Jacobs and Wills and the other great players of her era," King remembered. "Just being around her and hearing her talk about what it was like to play championship tennis under pressure, and about winning Wimbledon and Forest Hills, really rubbed off and gave me a sense of what it would be like for me when the time came."

Marble's illness was bothering her even then, in 1959. "She had to take oxygen every night," King recalled of weekends at Marble's home in Tarzana, California. "I'd hear her coughing in the next room."

Partly because of her illness—twice diagnosed as tuberculosis—Marble didn't play as well at Wimbledon during her peak years as she did at home because travel was often difficult. Partly too, though, it was because she wasn't above a certain theatricality that drained her concentration. She was like Tilden in this respect, although

Tilden in the midst of his temperamental posturings could also get his game together in a devastating way. Not so Marble.

"There was no question the gallery ate it up when they saw an attractive girl like Alice kick the ball after a bad shot or whack it into the backstop," Hazel Hotchkiss Wightman, the donor of the Wightman Cup, observed once. "But that's exactly where she was going wrong. She was thinking too much of the impression those displays were making on the galleries, and it was hurting her tennis."

Marble was distressed after dropping a 6–4, 6–4 match to Helen Jacobs in the Wimbledon semifinal in 1938, and asked Mrs. Wightman where she had gone wrong.

"You lost the match in the eighth game of the first set," Wightman said sternly. "You lost it when you began dramatizing yourself all over the court after you netted that drive, Alice—you know the one I mean. You were playing just as well as Helen. Let's see, you were behind 3–4 in games and you had 40–30 on your service. Then you netted that drive. You slipped on the shot and fell, right? What did you do then? You didn't brush off your shorts and get back into the match. No, you patted your fanny and you got a nice ripple of laughter from the gallery. So you continued to pat your fanny, and while you were amusing everyone you netted two more shots and tossed Helen the set. Your mind wasn't on your tennis. It took you *two full games* before you got back to business, and after that you never caught up. Even a girl with your natural equipment can't win if she allows *anything* to break her concentration."

Those sedate surroundings of old Wimbledon represented the farthest end of the spectrum from the land where Alice Marble climbed towering redwood trees as a youngster. Her father Harry married late in life, and when he did at thirty-nine he took his wife Jessie, a nurse in San Francisco, to a farm in a valley in the Sierra Nevada mountains in California's northeastern corner. As a single man Harry had worked in the forests as a high-climber, making his way with spurs and rope a couple of hundred feet above the ground to clear the tops from the tallest trees.

He was troubled by asthma and needed regular treatment in San Francisco. Once, a new nurse was in attendance at his doctor's office, Jessie Wood, who became his bride and the mother of five children: Dan, George, Hazel, Alice and Tim. By the time Alice was six she had learned to milk cows and ride horses and feed pigs and climb trees and collect fruit and vegetables from their gardens for Jessie to turn into preserves.

But the work was hard and the returns meager on the farm and in 1919 Harry Marble found a job with a lumber company in San Francisco and took his family there. Just before Christmas that year he was struck by a car, and in the hospital he developed pneumonia and died on Christmas eve. He left no insurance, and Alice's mother was compelled to rise seven days a week in pre-dawn hours to clean office buildings. The oldest boy, thir-teen-year-old Dan left school to take a job as a hardwood-floor apprentice to help his mother keep the family together. Alice's uncle Arthur, her mother's bachelor brother who was a brakeman on the cable cars, moved in with the family to help.

Arthur was a horse-player who taught Alice to read a

past-performance sheet. Sometimes she'd study his racing form and rate the thoroughbreds at San Francisco's top track, Golden Gate Fields, passing her best tips along to Uncle Arthur. Once, she spooked a longshot that returned $67 for a $2 bet. It kept the household in groceries for two weeks.

Uncle Arthur often took Alice and Dan and Tim to a corner lot to play ball. Alice was as good as any of them by the time she was thirteen. Meantime, brother George left school at fifteen to join Dan as a full-fledged hardwood-floor layer, with Dan gradually assuming a head-of-the-house role.

One weekend in early spring 1927 Uncle Arthur took the Marble kids to see the San Francisco Seals playing an exhibition ball game against Sacramento. A visiting player called to Alice sitting in the outfield seats, "Say, boy, how'd you like to climb down and play catch?"

When Alice realized he was speaking to her she was indignant, but not so indignant as to let it outweigh her desire to play. She hopped down and began to play a game of long pitch-and-catch with the outfielder. When the Seals took the field the players had been so impressed by Alice that Lefty O'Doul, their star outfielder who later went to the big leagues with the New York Giants, asked her to shag flies with him. It was a moment that came close to ranking with the emotion she felt on winning her first national tennis title a decade later. Next day a sportswriter on the San Francisco *Examiner* wrote a long piece about the thirteen-year-old girl shagging flies beside Lefty O'Doul.

The Seals provided passes for the Marble youngsters for weekend games that season, and on Sundays when the team was on the road the golden-haired flycatcher went to church with her mother. At Easter she sang a solo, her mother accompanying her at the piano, and on other Sundays she and brother Tim formed the battery for a team in Golden Gate Park, Alice pitching and Tim catching. Most evenings after dinner they went to a vacant lot near home.

"We had a special routine," Alice remembered. "First I practiced my fastball and curves while Tim caught, then in Tim's turn we stood about twenty feet apart while I bunted balls for Tim's infielding because he wanted to become a shortstop."

Even at fifteen with the contours of womanhood burgeoning, Alice had no thought of tennis. Her favorite schoolteacher, Betty Coyne, tried to interest her in this more ladylike pastime. Alice talked with a lisp and was shy in class when asked to read aloud. Betty Coyne kept her after school, taught her to speak without lisping and encouraged her to learn Irish clog dancing to help correct a pigeon-toed walk.

When Alice was five-feet-seven and 150 pounds, brother Dan decided it was time for her to act less like a male athlete. She was the mascot for the Seals, and Dan said she'd become too old for that too. He was half-hiding a tennis racquet as he spoke.

"Allie, you've got to stop being a tomboy," he told her. "I brought you this. Go out and play tennis."

Dan's admonishment was the turning point in Alice's life but she didn't know that then. "I was heartbroken," she remembered. "I went home and cried in bed all night."

With neighborhood kids hooting, Alice took her new

racquet down the street to the public courts of Golden Gate Park with their asphalt and concrete surfaces. They were the courts on which other noted players had begun their careers, Little Bill Johnston and Maurice McLoughlin, the California Comet of the pre-World War I era. The two Helens, Wills and Jacobs, played in their early days on those old asphalt courts, full of cracks and with no backgrounds except chicken wire.

Alice had a natural bent for the game. Her quick eye and athlete's reflexes brought early rewards. She made the school team, even beat a young man she secretly found attractive. She should have known better than to run him through the tennis hoops; he never spoke to her again.

Her brother Dan was anxious for her success. He used hard-earned income to enroll her at the California Tennis Club. She became a baby-sitter to get money to buy balls at thirty-five cents each. She worked in the cafeteria at the high school too, to help Dan's financial burden.

Through sheer acident, Alice became the candy-making champion of San Francisco's high schools. Her school cooking class had been assigned to make fudge, and working at home Alice couldn't get the ingredients to harden. Trying to salvage them, she and her mother buttered their hands, sat down facing one another and pulled the fudge like taffy. Gradually it hardened and as it did Alice braided it and set it to cool. It won a prize as the best candy in the class, and two days later was pronounced the best in all San Francisco.

There weren't many such high moments for young Alice. California Tennis Club members played in cliques,

75

seldom with newcomers and never with shy outsiders. She went to the club every day after school because Dan had paid $45 to make her a full-fledged junior member, but she rarely got a game. So she'd catch a streetcar back to the public courts and play with her friends. And they didn't always greet her with open arms—hadn't she gone a little high hat joining a private club?

But there was one rewarding and enduring result. A club member introduced her to a visitor from Los Angeles, one Harold Dickinson. They played long sessions of tennis and enjoyed each other's company over the succeeding weeks. And in the spring of 1931 when Alice was seventeen Dickinson introduced her to a tennis instructor from Los Angeles, Eleanor Tennant, who was conducting a clinic in San Francisco, and Tennant was to have a broad influence on her life.

In that summer of 1931 Marble "went East" for the first time, sent there by the California association as the junior champion of Northern California. She was knocked out in the first round of the singles and the doubles at Seabright, East Hampton and Rye by people she'd never heard of. She was frozen with fright in her first appearance at the nationals at Forest Hills, to her dismay drawn in the stadium in the first round, and she was quickly disposed of.

She sat discouraged in the stands watching a doubles match. A dark-haired woman approached, smiled and sat beside her. The woman said she could appreciate the disappointment. "I lost in the first round for three straight years," she said. She praised Alice's ability, encouraged her not to give up her enthusiasm for tennis, and advised her to study good players. "They don't rely on trick shots," the woman said. "You don't see Helen Wills or Helen Jacobs being fancy. They have command of three major shots, gained through years of practice."

Later, Alice pointed out the woman to her doubles partner, Bonnie Miller.

"Why, that's Mary K. Browne!" Bonnie exclaimed. "Do you *know* her?"

Alice said she knew her and, indeed, the three-time national singles champion had even offered to rally with her.

Alice went to Philadelphia for the national junior championships and reached the final. The humidity was high, she tired in all her matches. But stamina was not her only problem in the final where Ruby Bishop, a pupil of Eleanor Tennant's, beat her 6–3, 6–2. Marble ran to the locker room in tears, refusing to attend the presentation ceremony. When the woman who chaired the tennis committee, Mrs. Harrison Smith, went to the dressing quarters with Alice's medal, the youngster flung it across the room. "I don't want the damn thing," she cried.

She was accorded a patience she didn't deserve.

"We all have to learn to take hard knocks," Mrs. Smith said. "Some day, if you ever return to Forest Hills, look for the plaque with Kipling's words above the center court entrance:"

> *If you can meet with Triumph and Disaster*
> *And treat those two imposters just the same.*

Back in California Marble spent the winter working on her tennis game and helping brother Dan by getting a job in a bookstore. When she won the state championship in

77

1932 she qualified for the Eastern tournaments again. She was knocked out early at Rye, then went to Forest Hills to practice for two weeks for the nationals. She drew Sarah Palfrey, the fifth-seeded player, in the first round, and to her delight she beat her. She was eliminated by an English player but she and Marjorie Morill of Boston, unseeded and assuredly unsung, moved through round after round in the doubles to the final. There, they opposed Palfrey and Helen Jacobs, the top seeds, and played an excellent first set, losing 8–6. Jacobs and Palfrey ran out the second set but Marble returned to California encouraged by her showing. She lost in the final of the Pacific Southwest to Anna Harper, then beat Harper to win the Pacific Coast event a week later. At the end of all that and just turned nineteen she was ranked No. 7 in the U.S.

She was anxious to join Eleanor Tennant, remembering her trouble with Ruby Bishop in the junior final, and while she was pondering how, she got a phone call from Tennant who was impressed by that No. 7 ranking and invited her to stay with her in southern California. The family felt Alice was too young to leave home. Tennant then got her a job in San Francisco with the Wilson's sports equipment company and arranged for her to spend a month in L.A. two or three times a year for intensive coaching. Later, Tennant took her for instruction from Harwood (Beese) White, an architect devoted to the technique of tennis, who had worked with Helen Jacobs. Between them, White and Tennant remodelled Marble's game. In spite of her ranking she played like a tomboy grabbing a racquet and whaling away. She needed polishing; indeed, she needed reshaping—a different grip and better footwork.

Everything White suggested was opposed to the way Marble hit the ball. Her grip was a product of geography. California's concrete courts bounced the ball higher than clay or grass courts did. Instead of shaking hands with a racquet Californians usually placed the hand under it in the Western grip, making the stroke easier on high shots. Switching from the Western to the flat "shaking-hands" grip left Marble exasperated, barely able to control the ball, weak in her ground strokes with it.

Next, her instructors burdened her with books on technique by Wills, Lenglen, René Lacoste, Wilmer Allison and other stars. They were exasperating too. "They're not tennis books," she wailed. "They're anatomy books. They tell me where I put my elbow, what I do with my right foot. It's stupid!" In spite of her complaints and stubborn insistence that her coaches were wrong, she worked hard and gradually overcame the awkwardness of the new technique.

By July 1933 results began to emerge. Marble won the state championship again, and after she "went East" she won the Longwood and Essex tournaments, then lost in the Seabright semifinal to Sarah Palfrey who went on to beat Jacobs in the final. Only one tournament remained, a three-day invitation event at East Hampton on Long Island, before selection for Wightman Cup berths. Marble was dismayed to learn she'd been entered in both singles and doubles at East Hampton. She protested to Julian Myrick, the committee chairman. He was unmoved, even curt. "Mrs. Moody," he sniffed, referring of course to Helen Wills, the No. 1 player, "has afforded you the honor of playing with her in the doubles."

Marble suggested she withdraw from the singles, noting that Wightman Cuppers Palfrey and Carolyn Babcock were not playing in two events.

"We will be judge of who is to play—not you," Myrick told her.

On the tournament's third day Marble was in the semifinals of both singles and doubles. The first match at 10 o'clock was in singles against Midge Van Ryn, who took Alice to three long sets. The match had barely ended when she was advised that Wills was ready to play doubles. Three more long sets ensued during which Marble covered the backcourt for Wills on lobs. The champion's back was bothering her.

Next came the singles final, Marble against Betty Nuthall, former U.S. champion. The temperature had climbed to 104 degrees as Marble eked out the first set at 7–5. She lost the second, then found her muscles stiffening as she lay down in the locker room during a ten-minute rest period.

Nuthall ran out the third set over a weary opponent who, when it ended, made another clothes change for the doubles final. Myrick refused to default her, saying most spectators had come to watch Helen Wills Moody. So the match went on, and Marble lost there too. In addition, she dropped twelve pounds playing five matches—108 games in eleven sets—in a nine-hour ordeal on a blazing day. She fainted soon after leaving the court. She had a slight sunstroke and second-degree anemia.

This cost her a Wightman Cup place since a doctor

refused to permit her to play because of weakness. But she entered the nationals two weeks later and did well in early matches, reaching the semis opposite Betty Nuthall. She led 5–1 and 40–15 in the third set but couldn't score a winner on the two match points, then faded and lost at 7–5, and collapsed in the locker room.

That was the year Helen Wills defaulted in the third set to Helen Jacobs in the final. Watching from the stands, Marble was incensed when Wills gave up. "I knew Mrs. Moody's back had bothered her but if she could find the strength to walk to the clubhouse she could have played three more games," Marble observed later.

When the nationals ended she returned to California, ignoring the lingering fatigue, and worked hard with Eleanor Tennant whom she was now calling Teach, a name given the instructor by Hollywood actress Carole Lombard. Teach taught numerous movie stars, and once took Alice to a weekend party at William Randolph Hearst's castle at San Simeon where she enjoyed the company of movie people—Charlie Chaplin, Paulette Goddard, Bing Crosby, Constance Talmadge, Bebe Daniels and Ben Lyon, Marion Davies, director Raoul Walsh, Dorothy Mackail, Errol Flynn and Hearst columnist Arthur Brisbane.

Brisbane wrote of Marble in Hearst newspapers. "What a girl Alice Marble is, with everything the Venus de Milo has, plus two muscular, bare, sunburned arms marvellously efficient," he gurgled. "Her legs are like two columns of polished mahogany, bare to the knees, her figure perfect. Frederick MacMonnies should do a statue of her. And she should marry the most intelligent young man in America, and be the perfect mother with twelve children, not merely the world's best tennis player, which she probably will be."

Marble sailed for Europe with the Wightman Cuppers, going first to Paris. Her game was miserable and so was her mood. She was tired, the French language confused her, she was homesick, her muscles ached. She played the No. 2 French player Sylvia Henrotin in a daze. She heard the umpire say "quatre" and "un" and realized she was trailing 4–1. Next thing she knew she was awakening in a hospital bed, and she was in Neuilly. When Helen Jacobs visited her before departing for London and the Wightman Cup matches, Alice told her she could only remember a tennis ball that grew larger and larger until it looked as if it were about to crush her.

She was in pain from pleurisy but then Dr. Henri Dax bore her an infinitely more painful blow. "My dear girl, I'm afraid I have bad news for you," Dax said. "I'm afraid you have tuberculosis and may never play tennis again."

Two months later she was allowed to sail for New York where only two people greeted her, Eleanor Tennant and Marvin Moss, secretary of the USLTA. What Marvin wanted was for Marble to accompany him to the association offices immediately to submit a report of her expenses abroad. Teach pushed past him for a cab to the Roosevelt Hotel where she put her protégé to bed. A few days later Moss and Julian Myrick showed up from the association with a physician who studied X-rays from the French hospital and examined Marble. "This girl will never play tennis again," he reported.

Teach suggested to Myrick that the association pay future medical bills for Alice, as it had paid those in France.

When he refused, Tennant escorted him to the door. A week later, she took Alice home to California. Ten days after the joy of her homecoming, Alice wrote Teach to say she feared she was a burden on her mother who already had a house filled with family and work. Tennant arranged for Alice to move into a sanitarium near Los Angeles.

At twenty, Marble felt her life was over. She was miserable and lonely in spite of Teach's daily visits week after week. Then one morning she got a letter from the actress she admired immensely, Carole Lombard, one of Hollywood's brightest stars and a sensible person as well. "I'm a student of Teach Tennant's, you know," Carole wrote. "One day I was in a terrible automobile accident, and I found myself in a hospital bed for six months, just like you, with doctors saying I was finished. Well, I began to think I had nothing to lose by fighting, so I began to fight. I made my career come true, just as you can—if you'll fight."

The letter helped turn Marble around psychologically. She told Teach she wanted out of the sanitarium. She pulled on a sweater, piled on a coat and left, never to return. She was a blimp. She weighed 172 pounds.

She moved in with Teach and began looking after her instructor's correspondence, banking her money, making her appointments. Marble even planned her own recovery timetable.

"I would begin by walking a block or two a day until I could walk at least three miles," she wrote later of her regime. "When I was strong enough to do that, I would jump rope to build up the weak muscles in my legs. I would sing for an hour a day to build up my diaphragm muscles. I would read good books, books that would give a living working philosophy."

She grew close to Carole Lombard and the actress's brothers, Stew and Freddie, and their mother whom everyone called Petey. After a year Alice went to Dr. John Commons, a friend of Teach's who X-rayed her chest, studied her medical chart, probed and prodded and talked. At length he sat back. "You've never had tuberculosis," he said. "You've had pleurisy aggravated by anemia and that's all. You're now in first-class health. If you want to play tennis, I suggest you start by taking off thirty pounds while we're getting your anemia under control."

Marble went to Palm Springs where Teach was conducting clinics and when her weight was pared to 150 she began to take a few tentative swipes at a tennis ball. By the spring of 1936 she was down to 141 and rapidly showing the verve and dash in her serve-and-volley tennis game that had made her a glowing prospect two years earlier. By autumn there emerged the Alice Marble the tennis world soon came to know as one of the most exciting of players. She beat Helen Jacobs in the national final. Men turned their heads to watch.

# MAUREEN CONNOLLY

## [1934–1969]

No one knows the heights that might have been scaled by Maureen (Little Mo) Connolly had she not been marked by the unlikeliest of tragedies. At nineteen in 1954 and indisputably the queen of tennis, she was knocked from competition forever by a freak horse-riding accident, and in the prime of her life at thirty-four in 1969 she was a fatal victim of cancer.

Peter Wilson, a respected tennis critic in London, reflected in 1965 that it was the year Little Mo could be winning her *fourteenth* consecutive singles title at the Wimbledon championships. "She would still be only thirty by the time they were played," he reasoned. "Mrs. Moody, for instance, won Wimbledon for the eighth time when she was thirty-three."

Wilson remembered watching Little Mo beat Doris Hart in 1953 in what he described as the best women's singles final he ever witnessed at Wimbledon, but maintained that not he nor anyone else ever saw Mo at her best. "She still had a certain weakness on her service and with her volleying, on which she was still working," recalled this veteran of the London *Daily Mirror* who occasionally described himself as "the man they cannot gag" and "the world's greatest sportswriter." "I firmly believe

*Maureen Connolly*

that her greater speed about the court, her equal consistency and hitting power *plus* the reasonable supposition that she would have improved had her career continued, would have put Miss Connolly ahead of Mrs. Moody and would have gradually destroyed the gossamer touch of Mlle. Lenglen."

To be sure, Connolly compiled a tall record in her brief flicker. She won the U.S. singles title at sixteen in 1951 and repeated in 1952 and 1953. She never lost in singles at Wimbledon, winning there in 1952, 1953 and 1954. She won the French championship in 1953 and repeated in 1954, won in Australia in 1953 in her only visit there, and won the Italian in 1954.

And in 1953, a child of eighteen, Little Mo became the first woman to win the Grand Slam, the championships at Forest Hills and Wimbledon, in France and Australia. Nobody repeated until Margaret Court in 1970, and no one else has since.

After Connolly won her first U.S. crown in 1951 she lost only four matches anywhere—twice to Doris Hart, once to Shirley Fry, and once to Beverly Baker Fleitz who caught her in a California club's invitational tournament after a lengthy layoff and disposed of her handily, 6–0, 6–4. Otherwise, no one was close to Connolly who was getting ready for a fourth straight U.S. title when, in minutes, her career was over.

She had returned to her native San Diego in July 1954 after winning Wimbledon for a third time, stopping off at Chicago long enough to win a second U.S. national clay courts championship. The day after arriving in San Diego she went for a ride on her thoroughbred jumper, Colonel

Merryboy, a 1952 gift from home-town admirers. She was riding through Mission Valley near a roadway when her mount apparently was frightened by the approach of a cement-mixer truck. The horse slammed sideways against the truck, crushing Maureen's right leg. A bone was broken and tendons and muscles gashed and crushed. Surgery was unable to mend the leg entirely. Connolly's attorneys sued the concrete company on her behalf, charging the driver with negligence. Her career was over. She was awarded $110,734.

So who knows the ground Little Mo might have covered? It was apparent from her earliest tournament she was going somewhere. By sixteen she had won seventy-odd tournaments. Living across the street from the Balboa Park municipal courts in San Diego she started the game at ten, entered her first tournament a month later, and reached the finals. At fourteen she was the youngest player to win the national girls' championship, a title Helen Wills took at fifteen. When Mo turned fifteen she was ranked tenth among U.S. women players, and in June 1951, four months before she turned seventeen, she upset the sixth-ranked American, Nancy Chaffee, in the Southern California final.

By then Californians regarded her concentration as her most exceptional asset. Her ground strokes had almost equal rating. Perry Jones, the highest tennis authority in a region that produced top-flight players faster than avocados, appraised her as "the most remarkable young player to be developed in my thirty years in Southern California." Mo's coach, Eleanor (Teach) Tennant, who'd had a hand in the development of Alice Marble, Pauline Betz and Bobby Riggs, said Maureen was the best player

88

she'd ever drilled—"better than Wills and Marble at her age."

The surprise in Connolly's home state when she won over Chaffee was mild compared to the response she drew at Forest Hills in September. There, Doris Hart and Shirley Fry were solid favorites, the dominant players in Europe that summer. Fry had won the French singles shading Hart, and at Wimbledon Hart reversed it.

But at Forest Hills both were victimized by the five-foot-five, rosy-cheeked Connolly, a chunky young woman of 130 pounds with sun-streaked hair and the impassive concentration of the earlier Californian, Helen Wills. Mo eliminated Wimbledon champion Hart by 6–4, 6–4 in the semifinals, and then engaged in a nerve-shredding final with Shirley Fry. Indeed, as Allison Danzig, the gentleman from the *Times,* was to record: "The final was so nerve-wracking in the concluding stages, with the outcome hanging in the balance to the last stroke, that Miss Eleanor Tennant, Miss Connolly's coach, was near collapse at the end. She had to be administered to in a box in the marquee as her pretty little protégé let out a scream of joy and ran forward to greet her beaten opponent."

The match was a baseline duel. Fry played a waiting game, returning everything she could reach, hoping to tire Connolly in her hard-hitting style. It seemed to work too in the second set when Connolly began losing depth after a 6–3 first-set win. When Fry forced Maureen into a great deal of sideline-to-sideline running, she tired and her control broke and Fry ran out six straight games for a 6–1 margin.

Mo met her coach in the locker room at the interval.

"Oh, Teach, I'm so unsteady. I'm making all the errors!"

Tennant was firm and forceful. "You've got to be tough," she told her. "You've got to hang on, hang on with your eye teeth."

Back she went for the final set. In the eighth game, leading 4–3 and 40–15, she was one point from a 5–3 lead. But she failed on four successive shots and Fry tied the set. It was almost too much for Tennant on the sidelines.

But Mo broke Fry's service and went ahead 5–4 and then, on her own serve, she induced further anxiety upon her supporters with the match in her grasp, falling behind 15–40. She produced winners at this crucial stage, though, with an overhead, a drop shot and a backhand down the line. When Fry's return of serve on match point missed the line, Forest Hills had its youngest champion since May Sutton in 1905, three months younger than Connolly.

By then she was Little Mo to almost everyone, the name used first by Nelson Fisher of the San Diego *Union* for the battleship Missouri which also had notable fire-power on both sides.

But when Little Mo invaded England the summer of 1952 she presented a different figure than the girlish bobby-soxer who had squealed and cried for joy winning the U.S. title nine months earlier. British tennis fans were puzzled by the change. Far from bubbling and efferves-cent, the child prodigy they'd been reading about pre-sented herself as a stoic.

In this facade Connolly swept through the Manchester and Surbiton grass courts tournaments, creating news if she dropped even a game. She'd added occasional volleys and overheads to her devastating ground shots, but the grim demeanor turned off tennis buffs.

"The big thrill the Centre Court crowd so eagerly awaits, the defeat of the seventeen-year-old, much-vaunted American champion, is still to come," wrote Lance Tingay in the London *Daily Telegraph*. Teach Tennant was less than graceful in response. "She's out to kill them. You have to be mean to be a champion. How can you lick someone if you feel friendly toward them?"

Unperturbed on court, Connolly danced a little base-line jig, bobbing and always ready, running her opponents ragged with drives to the lines, occasionally rushing up to volley.

She met her rival from the Forest Hills final, Shirley Fry, in the semis and handled her more easily this time in straight sets. Her opponent in the final, Louise Brough, was nearly eleven years her senior, an American star who had won Wimbledon three years in a row 1948 through 1950, and had lost to Fry in the semifinal in 1951. Brough already held one win over Connolly, a month earlier in the Southern California final.

For this appearance Maureen was the delight of the bald and towering Teddy Tinling, the clothes designer, of whose creations it was often said no Wimbledon final could do without. She wore a full-sleeved cardigan of off-purple as she faced Brough, and she also wore her sphinx expression, working the court methodically, a blondish, plumpish automaton.

Mo won the first set 7–5, lost the opening pair of games in the second set and then settled into her groove for five straight games. Brough stayed the tide momentarily on a well-served game to climb to 5–3 but then Mo closed her out, and with the last point her stoicism gave way to a wild whoop.

"Whoopee!" cried Maureen Connolly, rushing to the net, her face aglow, to shake hands with the loser and then to accept her trophy of triumph from the Duchess of Kent. "Everything is just so wonderful," she gurgled later, her antics reflecting the Little Mo of Forest Hills a season earlier. "I'm all up in the air."

The father of Mo Connolly was a sailor who left the family when the child was three, and she was raised in San Diego by her mother and an aunt. Her mother had hopes to be a concert pianist but turned her dreams upon her daughter, pushing her into ballet and singing, and encouraging her to draw and write. None of these interested the youngster whose fancy—like that of a lot of little girls—was turned toward a fascination with horses. But there wasn't enough money to provide one, so the child instead focused her energy on the municipal tennis courts across the street.

She was ballgirl for the professional there, a man who hobbled on a wooden leg. Wilbur Folsom compensated for this physical handicap by developing marvellously co-ordinated ground strokes, which turned out to be his legacy to Connolly. There was another one too: she was left-handed when Folsom began to teach her, so one of his first acts was to switch her racquet to her right hand.

"For some reason, and you've got me what it is, women players don't make good tennis players if they're left-handed," he told her.

Maureen's mother's misdirected efforts to turn her daughter into a ballet dancer turned out to have a vital if indirect involvement in her development as a tennis star.

One of her dance instructors was acquainted with Eleanor Tennant, the accomplished tennis teacher, and observing Maureen's court skills this person asked Teach to take on the youngster as a pupil. Mo was twelve when she joined forces with Tennant who drove her hard. There were times when Maureen was upset and discouraged but she grew better by the week. Small wonder. She practiced three hours a day, five days a week, month upon month.

Tennant worked mostly on improving the ground strokes Wilbur Folsom had initiated. "It would have been brutal to teach a little girl a spectacular service," Tennant reflected once. "She needed her strength to grow. She's *little.*"

With all the work, Connolly still managed to keep up her grades at Cathedral Catholic High School in San Diego, though travelling often to tournaments. She was the youngest person to win the junior championships of Colorado, Utah, Washington, Arizona, Southern California and the Pacific Southwest. She won the national junior crown without loss of a set and, entering adult competition, travelled to Canada and became the youngest winner of the British Columbia women's singles. *American Magazine* described her as "an all-round player with a strong forehand and terrific ability to concentrate . . . deceptively unspectacular with a racquet," resembling seven-time champion Helen Wills "in strength, stamina and complete lack of expression no matter how the game goes." As early as 1948 when Maureen had just turned fourteen, Al Laney, the knowledgeable tennis writer for the New York *Herald-Tribune,* centered upon her skills as those "belonging to someone who is headed towards the

93

stars." As though to make him a prophet she climbed to tenth in national rankings at fifteen.

At sixteen in 1951, the year of her graduation from high school, she was picked on the Wightman Cup team and won eight adult tournaments in a row, beating players seeded nationally ahead of her, such as fourth-seeded Beverly Baker twice, sixth-seeded Nancy Chaffee four times, fifth-seeded Pat Todd, seventh-seeded Betty Rosenquest and ninth-seeded Helen Perez once each. She lost only twice—to Pat Todd in the Eastern grass courts championships and to Wimbledon champion Doris Hart in the semifinal at Brookline, Massachusetts. In her Wightman Cup match she dropped only four games to England's Kay Tuckey.

When Connolly went to Forest Hills for the nationals she swept through to the final without losing a set. She engaged Shirley Fry in the match that almost caused Teach Tennant to faint. Indicating what a cool little cucumber she'd become, Mo told Tennant when Teach's emotions had returned to normal: "Now we can go home and work on the offensive game."

Back home she said goodbye to formal education and got a job on the San Diego *Union* as a copy girl to earn money for a wardrobe for Wimbledon in 1952. Apart from that, every energy belonged to tennis. She gave up swimming because it might develop the wrong muscles and movies because they might strain her eyes. The only outside interest she retained was horse riding, which she adored. On the tennis court her style distinguished her from most women players. Nimbly dancing on the baseline, up on her toes always, she'd stop suddenly, bounce into position and lean into backhand or forehand

94

scorchers, then bob expectantly at the baseline again. Like all champions, her sense of anticipation was acute.

After she won at Wimbledon in 1952 and repeated at Forest Hills, she prepared for a run at the Grand Slam by heading for Australia in December for the opening tournament of the 1953 season. Almost immediately a controversy arose. The women players Down There turned sour toward Mo for not practicing with them, "hitting up" with Aussie men instead. They were critical too that she was picking up tips from the czar of Australian tennis, Harry Hopman. Though the Davis Cup team's captain, Hopman helped her when he couldn't be bothered showering wisdom on Aussie women players. "We don't learn much by watching her beat our players, but we might if we had an opportunity of practicing with her and picking up Harry Hopman's tips that way," one player complained, reflecting the general mood.

Launching her season there, Little Mo nearly swept the boards in the Australian national championships. She beat Margaret Hawton 6–2 and 6–1 in the singles semifinals and then easily handled her American compatriot Julie Sampson in the final with loss of five games. She and Sampson won the doubles without losing a set, and she and Ham Richardson went to the finals in the mixed. Aussie Rex Hartwig and Sampson stopped them there, though, in straight sets.

Next the French. Every time Little Mo looked up on a tennis court in Paris, there was Doris Hart. They met in the final round of the singles, the doubles and the mixed, and Hart was the winner twice. But not in the big one, the singles, where Mo prevailed 6–2 and 6–4. Hart and Shirley Fry won from Connolly and Julie Sampson in straight sets in the doubles and Hart and Vic Seixas shaded Mo and Australia's Mervyn Rose in a three-set mixed final.

Which brings the cast of characters to Wimbledon. By then Connolly was halfway to the Slam. She zipped through to the final at England's tennis shrine, demolishing Shirley Fry in the semis 6–1, 6–1. So once again, here she was facing Doris Hart, one of the subtlest and most graceful competitors, who had turned twenty-eight that June and was, accordingly, nearly a decade more experienced than her countrywoman, the kid across the net.

The match was perhaps the only difficult one Maureen Connolly ever encountered in a big tournament. But in the end, she had the skills and fervor to make key points at vital moments, as she came away with 8–6 and 7–5 margins in two strenuous and emotionally draining sets. Hart got a measure of consolation in the doubles final when she and Shirley Fry stunned Little Mo and Julie Sampson. They didn't lose a game in a two-set shutout, perhaps unique in the annals of Wimbledon finals.

In singles, though, only Forest Hills remained for Mo's sweep two months later. They were months fraught with controversy; yes, fraught with controversy. The little lady declined to play the grass events at Merion and South Orange, and tennis writers turned savage in the New York dailies, charging that Mo had grown snobbish and overburdened with her own importance. "National Champion Giving Net Fathers Hard Time with Prima Donna Act," one paper headed a lengthy piece of criticism. Another journal went to its editorial page to suggest that the USLTA give Little Mo a lesson in modesty. There was enough furor that Connolly was moved to write a Sunday-supplement rebuttal entitled "I Am No Swell-Head." She'd stayed out of the tournaments, she said in this piece, because she was overly tired after Wimbledon and needed rest. There wasn't much doubt that she suspected some criticism was justifiable, though. She apologized for specific incidents. "I may have become irritated with some particular photographer who got too close while I was serving or running for a wide ball," she wrote. "And I don't like to be asked questions when I'm all keyed up before or after a match. Give me fifteen minutes to calm down and I can answer."

On the court she had all the answers. She whipped poor Shirley Fry 6–1, 6–1 in the semifinals, a duplicate of Wimbledon, and once again she faced Doris Hart in a final round. Doris was near the top of her game this time too, handling Louise Brough in straight sets in her half of the semis.

But the final was all Connolly. As Allison Danzig reported in the *Times,* "In forty-three minutes Miss Connolly, with her devastating speed and length off the ground and showing vast improvement since last year, took the match 6–2, 6–4. Miss Hart, a finalist five times and a strong hitter in her own right, resorted to every device, including changes of spin, length and pace, in an effort to slow down her opponent. But Miss Connolly went implacably on to victory in one of her finest performances."

By 1954 Maureen Connolly was moving from peak to peak. She won in Rome for the second time and went on to Paris to take the French again (and teamed with a couple of Aussies, Nell Hopman and Lew Hoad, to capture the doubles titles too) and was as devastating as ever

97

at Wimbledon, beating Louise Brough in straight sets in the final. By now even the severest of critics was regarding her as an all-time all-timer though not yet twenty. Lance Tingay of the *Daily Mail* reflected upon this in a book in 1977, the year of Wimbledon's centenary. "Miss Connolly's backhand drive was assuredly the fastest and most accurate shot of its kind ever played by a woman," he wrote. "What position she should occupy among the all-time greats is necessarily a matter of opinion, but that Miss Connolly ranks among them is certain."

Dominating the field after that 1954 Wimbledon, she would almost certainly have added a fourth straight U.S. title had not the riding accident ended her career in July that summer. She had hoped to resume tennis upon recovery, probably as a professional, but her injury was more serious than was thought and she announced her retirement in February 1955. Later that year Little Mo married Norman Brinker, a San Diego businessman and former member of the United States Olympic equestrian team, and in time they had two daughters, Cindy and Brenda.

The family moved to Dallas where the former queen of tennis became active with the Maureen Connolly Brinker Foundation for the advancement of tennis achievement among junior players in Texas. Explaining her inability to play tournaments though able to instruct on the court, she said her strokes were as good as they had ever been but that she had a problem of mobility. "If the ball is out of reach I have to let it go," she said a little sadly. But she recovered quickly. "I've had a full life with lots of travel and I've met lots of wonderful people. Now I'm a housewife. It's a new career and I'm awfully happy with it."

But in 1966 she became ill with cancer. She battled it for three years, losing ground and coming back and losing ground again. On June 21, on the eve of the 1969 Wimbledon, she lost that one.

*Margaret Smith Court*

# MARGARET SMITH COURT

## [1942-        ]

$\mathcal{M}$ARGARET SMITH COURT, a tall paradox, won enough major championships across the face of the globe in the 1960s and early 1970s to tax a computer. Strangely, however, the lasting impression of this sinewy Australian is that she would fade under pressure—that she'd "do an el foldo," as her arch rival Billie Jean King occasionally phrased it.

Court's record overshadows everyone's who ever knocked a backhand down the line. She won her own country's singles championship before she turned eighteen in 1960, and by the time she'd turned thirty-one she'd added exactly *sixty* titles in the world's four major tournaments alone—the Australian, the French, Wimbledon and Forest Hills. Those sixty-one championships in singles, doubles and mixed doubles made countryman Roy Emerson's runnerup mark of twenty-eight Big Four titles look puny.

She won the Grand Slam in 1970, an achievement shared only with Maureen Connolly. She made a shambles of competition in her native land, winning the singles championship down there eleven times. Also, she lay waste to the U.S. and the French titles with notable frequency—five times each—and on three occasions got to curtsy to the royal box at Wimbledon as the champion of that ancient shrine in London's outer reaches.

As tournaments attracting the toughest fields, those were the most prestigious scalps. Now add a net full of lesser national crowns as side dishes: the Italian three times, the German three times, the South African twice and the Canadian once, totalling thirty-three national singles titles. Next, there are something like fifty major doubles and mixed doubles baubles, and an additional galaxy of invitational and indoor romps to produce a cornucopia of silver cups and folding bills. One year, after over-the-counter payment replaced under-the-table payoffs, she reeled in $205,000. That was in 1973 when the big money was just beginning to shower upon women's tennis.

In spite of all this, though, Margaret Smith Court could never really shake the widespread notion that she was likely as not to choke in important matches. This wasn't only in the U.S. where she had white-lipped rivalries with King and Darlene Hard and with the adored Brazilian Maria Bueno and where a certain testiness could be expected; no, it was in good old fair-play England, as well.

Indeed, where it began was at Wimbledon and perhaps it was unfair because Margaret Smith was a youngster not yet nineteen the first time she set foot there. Still, she was already a ranking internationalist, twice champion in Australia, semifinalist in Rome, quarterfinalist in Paris and the winner of two English grass court events leading to Wimbledon. So the English press made her No. 1 for the big event in screaming headlines.

She met England's unseeded Christine Truman in the fourth round on Centre Court. They split the first two sets, then Smith jumped ahead 4–1 in the deciding one. Unexpectedly, Truman got back into the match, forcing extra games at 5–5. She seemed done in when Smith pinned her at 6–5 and 40–15 but somehow Margaret netted volleys on each of the two match points, and in the long run Truman pulled out the match at 9–7. That started talk of Centre Court Jitters and the words greeted Margaret when she returned a year later wearing a third Aussie title and the championships of Italy and France as well.

"The English newspapers were the worst source of pressure," she reflected in her autobiography, *Court on Court,* in 1975. "I couldn't open one without reading about 'Smith's Centre Court Nerves.' Everywhere I went reporters asked me if I would be 'nervy' against Billie Jean. There was no escaping. I had earned a reputation for big-match jitters at Wimbledon the year before that I couldn't live down."

And she didn't live it down in that June 1962 against brash and aggressive Billie Jean, an unseeded outsider. In later years King often called herself the Old Lady but in truth she was a year and four months younger than Smith, a rookie on the English circuit, though No. 3 in the U.S.

They met in the second round on a cold windy day and Centre Court was surrounded by 12,000 chilly and intense faces as they squared off. Smith whistled to a 6–1 win in the opening set because Billie Jean was feeling a little stage fright herself. She squared the match via 6–3, though, and then the favored Smith rushed ahead 5–2 in the third. She dropped Billie Jean's serve for 5–3, then quickly got a 40–15 edge on her own. Two match points.

Gutsy Billie Jean took four straight points for the game, won her own serve, broke Margaret again for a 6–5 lead and then got to match point three times before finally submerging the Aussie at 7–5.

"I had to fight back tears of humiliation," Smith recounted. "That was the start of the personal rivalry between Billie Jean and myself . . . and [it] plunged me into the deepest despondency of my life." She recovered quickly enough when hundreds of people sent messages or made personal calls and when Fred Perry, England's one-time world champion, wrote an open letter of cheer in a London newspaper. "There is always another day and at the age of nineteen, with a tennis game such as yours to back you up, the good days will far outnumber the bad," part of his piece said.

Over the years Court and King met all across the globe, indoors and out, and in all seasons and climates. By 1973 Margaret had won more than her share—twenty-one to Billie Jean's thirteen—and had eradicated much of her reputation as a choke artist. But that's the year it went sky high for all time; that's the year she fell into the web spun by the rascally Robert Riggs. Riggs had offered to bet Billie Jean he could beat her for $5000, winner take all, but she'd brushed him off. He threw the same bait to Margaret (it was subsequently doubled) and she could hardly wait to swallow it.

They played at San Diego on Mother's Day, and as Bobby modestly phrased it after he'd psyched her silly and trounced her in straight sets: "I had become the hero of all middle-aged men smarting under the taunts of the Women's Libbers, the leader of Bobby's Battalions, and the undisputed No. 1 male chauvinist in the world."

Of course he had. And all because Court had blown all semblance of cool at a moment when she was undisputed queen of women's tennis. In that spring of 1973, about six months after her return to tennis following the birth of her first child, she had won twelve tournaments in a row, including four Virginia Slims events in the States. Her feeling about the match, she said upon accepting the challenge from the 55-year-old hustler, was that as the best player in the world she should defend women's tennis against Riggs and his insults. Putting down arch-rival King she noted that she was beating her consistently on the Slims circuit "whenever she wasn't pulling out of these events."

Court claimed she regarded the Riggs match as "a kind of breather for me on the women's tour." It never occured to her that Riggs would give her trouble, she reflected, and she had no idea the match would capture people's imaginations all around the world. But it did, and practically everybody joined in the argument over the sexes.

She could hardly have performed worse. "I played the match in a daze and it remains mercifully foggy to me in retrospect," she was to reflect. "I knew Riggs's shots would be weak, but not *that* weak." Bad as he was, she was worse. She double-faulted frequently, hit waist-high shots beyond the baselines, and overheads into the net. Riggs won the match, laughing all the way, 6–2, 6–1.

"I guess the Good Lord was not on my side that day," Court wrote in her book, touching on another dominant side of her life on court. As a deeply religious woman, raised a Roman Catholic and devout all through her career, she called on God at critical moments in matches

("Please, God, help me now!") and always prayed before big matches. She believed her tennis talent came from God "and was meant to serve a purpose. I feel God *gifted* me".

In 1976, nearing thirty-four, she said she was considering retiring because she was "having visions on the palms of my hands." She said they were of a religious theme and lasted about two minutes. "I think I have been selected by the Lord to do something very special in life. The Lord is strengthening, showing, and teaching me the way."

A few months later, at home in Perth, she said she was through with tennis. "If I had been meant to play God would have led me to it."

By then, Margaret Smith Court had been at or near the international pinnacle for seventeen years, a tall achievement for a person from a family of no athletic bent in the country town of Albury. It was on the border of the two states New South Wales and Victoria, where her father was foreman of the ice cream section of the local milk and cheese plant. This made her leader of "the Smith Gang"—all boys except her—a lean lithe tomboy climbing trees and playing cricket and football and, her favorite game, tennis. The Smith home was one of a row facing on the Albury and Border Lawn Tennis Association with twenty-five grass courts.

Margaret was the youngest of four children, though in a sense an only child. The oldest, Kevin, was born in 1929, and Vincent and June in the next three years. Margaret came along on July 16, 1942, ten years after June's arrival. She and her father were close, especially in their love of fishing, sitting quietly in a rowboat on the Murray River, drifting gently.

Margaret began playing tennis on the road between her house and the Albury courts, using grass-stained tennis balls that bounced past the club's hedges or into them. Her racquet was a long thin board until she was eight when a friend of her mother's recalled owning an old one that she resurrected and gave her. It had a square head, no leather on the grip, and numerous broken and loose strings. It was better than a long thin board, but not much.

Margaret and three boys her age crawled under the fence surrounding the club after school and played on a court partially hidden from clubhouse view by a thick hedge. The only way they could be seen was if a ball hit the backstop, so Margaret stood at the net and the others along the baseline banging the ball at her. She cut off shots so the ball wouldn't hit the backstop, and when she became a world-class player and people applauded her exceptional volleying skill she told them it was the first stroke she ever learned.

In those later years, it was hard to miss Margaret at the net. She was called The Arm by little Rosie Casals because "when Margaret comes to the net all you can see is that big right one reaching in every direction." A laboratory in London tested Court once and found her arms were three inches longer than most women's of her height. Also, her right-hand grip strength measured 121½ pounds, unusual for a woman.

In Grace Lichtenstein's book, *A Long Way, Baby*, the point is made that in action Court's appearance "seemed to transform itself from minute to minute," and, indeed, as anyone who saw her play will recall, there was a startling transformation the moment Margaret stopped leaping and diving and hammering for a point. Once it ended, as Lichtenstein observes, "She would straighten her shoulders, raise her head as if an invisible crown were being placed on it, stare straight ahead and walk slowly, regally, back to position. You could almost hear 'Pomp and Circumstance.' Margaret Court carried herself like a queen."

There was none of this in Margaret Smith, the leggy Aussie beginner belting a ball against the wall of a brick garage in Albury or swinging at one suspended on a string from her backyard tree. She was a natural left-hander but heard so many taunts she switched. In later years she blamed the change for chronic problems with her serve. Also, she reflected that she always enjoyed hitting backhands more than forehands, an unusual preference among tennis players. The great Australian player Ken Rosewall was also a natural left-hander who switched, whose backhand was his superior stroke, whose serve was a problem that wouldn't go away.

Tennis was the booming sport in Austrialia in the post World War II years when Davis Cuppers Rosewall and Lew Hoad were national heroes. Margaret, at nine, enrolled with 150 other kids in that tiny town where she grew up eager to become an internationalist like the Davis Cuppers. The fee was two shillings a week, less than half a dollar, to learn to hit the ball properly.

She kept growing and playing—and losing—through her early and middle teens. Her nemesis was Jan Lehane, coached by Vic Edwards whose later famous protégé was

Evonne Goolagong. Lehane had a two-handed backhand in the 1950s that gave Court as much difficulty as Chris Evert's ever did in the early 1970s. Margaret couldn't handle Lehane until she was seventeen, losing in every tournament they played for five years.

By then Margaret had moved from little Albury to Melbourne where the one-time Davis Cupper Frank Sedgman hired her in his office. She did shorthand and typing. Sedgman turned her over to a leading coach Keith Rogers for tennis instruction. He'd call for her at 6:30 in the morning at a room she shared with her sister Jill, and he'd run with her in a nearby park for an hour before she went to work. Then he'd work on her tennis game every afternoon. Sedgman directed her to a gymnasium he owned in Melbourne to build her physique. She'd dress quickly before men arrived, then compete with them in running and exercising and even weight-lifting under an instructor named Stan Nicholes, who became a close friend and invaluable adviser in remedying numerous injuries all through her career. When they first met Nicholes devised exercises to strengthen her wrists and fingers and forearms, others to develop back muscles for serving, smashing and springing, and others for ankle and calf muscles. He gave her a program for running too and she pursued fitness as long as she competed.

Still, she was no muscle moll. Though she worked painstakingly to develop physically she was always conscious of wanting to look feminine (accounting, obviously, for the on-court transformation that amused Lichtenstein). She took dressmaking courses at school and when she later got her hands on tennis money she went to the two leading designers of women's tennis clothes, Britishers Teddy Tinling and Fred Perry, the old champ, for her court wear.

In 1962 Tinling flew into a snit when Smith decided she didn't like his frilly creations and switched to Perry's tailored designs. Teddy, who had produced the famous lace-edged panties worn by Gussie Moran at Wimbledon in 1949, didn't speak to Margaret for ten years after she opted for Perry. Then they became compatible again when she joined the Virginia Slims circuit in 1972.

Working hard in the gymnasium and on the court, Smith endlessly sought to improve her game through her mid-teens in Melbourne. She lived with the Sedgmans—though she never did feel at ease with Frank, her first employer—and helped Jean Sedgman with the four Sedgman children when she wasn't lifting weights or running or hitting tennis balls.

When she was seventeen she sprouted on court over-night. She lashed old rival Jan Lehane for the first time ever in a state tournament preceding the Australian nationals. There she was seeded seventh, well back of No. 1, Maria Bueno of Brazil, the Wimbledon champion and Forest Hills winner whom Margaret had played in the South Australian championships in January. She was so awed she could scarcely concentrate ("I was completely mesmerized by her dark beauty, her lovely tennis frock, and the fact she was the Wimbledon champion") and won only three games.

But after beating Lehane, Margaret felt differently because Lehane had beaten Bueno once. In her methodical way Margaret concluded that if Lehane could do this, she could too.

So in that frame of mind Smith faced the champion in

the quarterfinals of the Australian nationals ("I was so filled with anticipation I could hardly wait for our match to begin"). There were 3000 people there, the largest crowd she'd ever stepped in front of. In stifling heat she played as one possessed, running down every ball, swinging out on all her shots, rushing the net at every opening. She won the first set 7–5 and jumped ahead 3–1 in the second.

And then Bueno, all but swept away by the feverish youngster, brought the skills to play that had taken her to championships in New York and London, and won five straight games to square the match.

Refreshed by a shower during a ten-minute interval, Margaret got her volleys under control and assumed a 5–2 lead. Nonplussed that the unknown had regained the initiative, Bueno dug in once more, held serve, broke Smith's, and prepared to tie the match at 5–5 as she toed the service line.

Perhaps Maria let down, for she was soon behind, serving at 15–40. She drilled a volley winner to climb to 30–40 but when Smith sent her wide for a forehand, Maria's shot caught the net. She didn't speak as she shook Smith's hand, and was in tears when Smith got to the dressing room after being delayed by the newshounds. "She didn't speak to me then or at any time before she left Australia," Smith recounted. "I was shocked that a world champion could behave so badly in defeat. It was a lesson to me. I was beginning to realize the enormous pressures on the top player to keep on winning and, more important, not to suffer a bad loss, a loss to an unknown."

Margaret and Maria didn't hit it off after that, meeting

frequently in tournaments around the world as grim stoics. They played twenty-three times before the oft-injured Bueno retired for a time in 1969, and Court won sixteen.

She followed that first surprising win by eliminating defending champion Mary Reitano in the semifinals, and opposite her in the final was Jan Lehane, who was stern opposition in the first set, won by Smith at 7–5, but none whatever in the second, 6–2, and Margaret became the youngest singles winner ever in her native country.

She made her first overseas tour that summer. Halfway through the French championships she was stricken by an illness that recurred regularly. At Wimbledon she was sped from the dressing room to a hospital one evening; the illness that had been draining her for weeks was diagnosed as glandular fever. When she was released six weeks later her weight had dropped from 145 to 133. She revived enough to play in her first American championships, working through to the semifinals where she and the defending champion Darlene Hard launched a rivalry that ensued for three years and was even more white-lipped than the one with Maria Bueno. Darlene prevailed in three sets and went on to win the back-to-back national championships. Margaret returned home to work on her backhand's topspin, to turn that shot into a real game-breaker. Which she did.

That winter the Australian association imported Hard for tournaments. The rivalry with Smith grew as the young Aussie kept knocking off the American champion—in four straight tournaments leading to the nationals down there. In the big one, Hard was kayoed by Jan Lehane in the semifinals. Smith toyed with Lehane at love and two in a thirty-five minute final. Hard couldn't get out of the country fast enough, vowing she'd fix Smith when she got her in the States.

Heading overseas again, Margaret became the first Aussie to win the Italian title, a sweat-soaked marathon with Maria Bueno at 8–6, 5–7 and 6–4. Then she won her first French championship—and, again, the first for an Australian—at the Roland Garros Stadium, taking countrywoman Lesley Turner in a three-set final in which Turner held match point at 5–3 and 40–30. Smith went right after her, though, and won the next four games for the championship.

Never mind that courage, the English papers were on Smith's back with the Centre Court Jitters theme when she arrived for Wimbledon. This was the tournament in which Smith was smitten in the second round by Billie Jean, making the newshounds prophetic. Heading for America after that failure Margaret turned twenty crossing on the *Queen Elizabeth*. King was not a problem at Forest Hills but two of Smith's other arch-enemies were— Bueno and Hard (there rarely seemed to be a major tournament when poor old Margaret wasn't surrounded by people jealous of her or who resented her). She met the Brazilian in the semis and shaded her in a marvellous match 6–8, 6–3, 6–4, and that sent her in against Darlene.

"Darlene was not above resorting to gamesmanship, but she pulled a new trick in this match which nearly cost me the title," hard-done-by Margaret recalled later. What happened was that with Smith holding a 4–2 lead in the wake of a 9–7 first-set edge, Hard complained about a late call by a linesman. The linesman held firm, wounding Darlene.

"Instead of going on with the game, the American walked to the backstop, dropped her racquet, put her head in her hands and began to sob loudly," Smith recounted. "I had never seen anything quite like it. To the embarrassment of everyone watching, Darlene went on crying, and I sat down on the grass court to wait until the tears stopped flowing."

When the Niagara was stayed, Hard tied the set at 4-4, then lost two games in a row for the match. That made Margaret the first Australian woman to wear the American crown, her third win of the four Grand Slam tournaments that year. Winning three of four became a habit, in fact, and contributed to Billie Jean's el foldo label. She did it four times in all—1962 (all but Wimbledon), 1965 (all but the French) and 1969 and 1973 (both years all but Wimbledon). So she missed out somewhere along the trail four times in five chances.

In 1970, though, she brought it off, the only woman apart from Maureen Connolly to win the Slam in a year. By then she had met and married the tall and amiable Aussie Barry Court, a sailing enthusiast, son of Sir Charles Court, accountant and politician, once premier of Western Australia. Between wedding bells and the successful Grand Slam, Margaret took fourteen months off, initially planning to retire from the grind. But the idea of touring with Barry, showing him the places she was familiar with around the world, encouraged her to return to the circuit late in 1967. It required close to a year of tournaments to get back the winning edge.

By 1969 she was in full sail, winning her eighth Australian crown, her third French and her third American. In between she blew Wimbledon, knocked off by fourth-seeded Ann Haydon Jones, British lefthander who went on to beat Billie Jean King in the final, both in three sets and both surprises.

So, searching for the Slam, the Courts embarked on their third world tour in 1970, and Barry got a clear idea of the grind his wife endured. In three months they covered four continents. On the indoor circuit in the U.S. she beat Billie Jean in the finals at Philadelphia and Dallas, then flew to Australia where Billie Jean beat her in Sydney, then flew to South Africa where she beat Billie Jean. Now to England a week after that and the realization by Margaret that her game was off kilter. What to do? Get on an airplane, of course, and fly somewhere. This time to Los Angeles for a week of coaching with Jerry Teaguarden, who made small changes in the serve and forehand shots. Then to Paris for the French championships where all that bothered her were muscle spasms, a blood clot, and Olga Morozova, the Russian champion. Olga threatened to end Slam hopes in the second round. Implacable and patient on the slow French clay of Roland Garros, Morozova had Court down 6–3 and 5–2.

Rushing the net on every exchange Margaret won that second set 8–6, managing to develop a leg cramp that knotted the calf muscle into a tight ball. Desperate to end the match, she ran out a 6–1 third set, then learned the cramp had caused a clot in the calf muscle, which in turn went into a spasm. Next morning she couldn't get out of bed. But she wasn't scheduled to play so she took pain-reducing tablets and muscle-relaxing massage. Instead of incapacitating her, the injury made her even more devastating on the court. "I feel I have to win every point to last the match," she explained once. So when concentration and determination reach their zenith Margaret became a terror.

In this fashion she got through to the final without dropping a set and handled Helga Masthoff Niessen there, hardly taking a deep breath. This was her second leg on the Slam, and her fourth French championship (she made it five in 1973, second only to Suzanne Lenglen's six).

At Wimbledon in June, out came the headlines: *Is Margaret Going to Freeze?* She was seeded No. 1, as always and in spite of the headlines, and Billie Jean was No. 2. Both performed to justify the seedings in the early rounds, but in the fourth Court went up against another injury and a different Helga Niessen (for a while anyway). Margaret was trailing 7–6 in the opener when she leaped at a passing shot and fell and landed on her left ankle which twisted under her falling weight. She hobbled through the next game, lost it and the set at 8–6, and sent a ballboy for an elastic ankle pad to provide a semblance of support. The ankle was swelling, changing color and increasing in pain as the second set began, so Court had to bear down if she were going to last. Whammo! She knocked off the helpless rival across the way by 6–0 and 6–0, indicating that the ankle *really* hurt.

She decided to concentrate everything on physical survival. She cancelled mixed doubles and women's doubles commitments with Marty Reissen and Judy Dalton and dragged her badly discolored ankle and aching foot to a doctor. "You've torn the ligaments and the foot has hemorrhaged," the man said.

The cancellations gave her two off days. With constant

ice-pack applications and rest she made it to her semifinal match with Rosie Casals. An injection would have killed the pain for two hours, so she went to work on little Rosie in order to complete the execution in less than those 120 minutes. She rushed the net on her serve and on Rosie's too, and she put aside the tiny Californian in just under ninety minutes, 6–4 and 6–1, giving herself half an hour's smiling time before the foot and ankle resumed their throb. Then more treatment from the doctor, more ice packs and more rest for the twenty-four hours preceding her match with Billie Jean in the final. King had dumped Francoise Durr, the French retriever, 6–3 and 7–5 in her half of the semis.

The King-Court match turned out to be one of the all-time all-timers. Luckily for Court, her physician phoned the house doctor at Wimbledon and advised him to give Margaret a double shot of pain-killer. If he hadn't, she would not have lasted because the match turned out to be the longest women's final ever at Wimbledon, two hours and twenty-seven minutes, and although it went only two sets it encompassed forty-six games, almost the equivalent of four sets at 7–5.

In the first set Court showed amazing calm and determination in the face of her Centre Court Jitters reputation to square the score three times when Billie Jean was serving for the set. This happened with King ahead at 5–4, then at 7–6, and then at 8–7. When Margaret leveled the count at 8–8 by breaking serve for the third time, Billie Jean smashed her racquet to the sacred sod of dear old Wimbledon, breaking the frame in frustration.

So on went the marathon through nine more games, each holding service until the score reached 13–12, Court leading and King serving. Here, B.J. made three errors in a row. Court was thereby vaulted to a 14–12 edge. The set had consumed ninety minutes. The second one picked up in precisely the same pattern. If one held serve, so did the other; if a service break were forced by one, the other came back to force an equalizer. It went that way for nineteen games at which point Court led 10–9 on King's serve, and Court kept forcing a match point and B.J. kept fighting her off. Five times Margaret needed one more point, and four times Billie Jean foiled her. But not five times, and Court brought if off at 11–9.

That should have ended the stigma of the choke, and it should certainly have been rendered DOA when Court finished off her Grand Slam sweep a couple of months later at Forest Hills with a three-set win over Casals (King had undergone knee surgery following the finale at Wimbledon and missed the U.S. nationals that autumn). Completing the Slam brought long-sought recognition for Margaret, but then came the pest, Bobby Riggs, in 1973 and that weird interlude provided the el foldo image that followed her to the end of her days on court.

# ALTHEA GIBSON

## [ 1927–      ]

$I$ T'S NEXT TO IMPOSSIBLE to measure the distance travelled by Althea Gibson from the soiled sidewalks of New
York's Harlem to the impeccable manicure of the lawns
at Wimbledon—something on the order of 3500 miles
plus one light year.

In the comparative enlightenment of the late 1970s,
the prejudice endured by black athletes a mere twenty
years earlier is almost forgotten—or at least the extent of
it is. All through the 1970s in the playpens of the western
world black was beautiful. When Althea Gibson was
emerging from the ghetto two decades or so earlier, black
was anything but. Indeed, even the word was unusual; in
the 1950s blacks were called coloreds or Negroes or much
worse.

So when Gibson was starting out, most clubs wouldn't
accept her entry and wouldn't admit her person. Some of
the world's stuffiest bigots gravitated toward tennis, people who would as soon throw their tournaments open to
circus clowns as to blacks—sooner, if the clowns happened to be white Anglo-Saxon Protestants.

But even beyond her color Gibson was an unlikely can-
didate for success at Wimbledon and Forest Hills. She
was a wild, arrogant kid growing up in Harlem, playing

*Althea Gibson*

stickball and basketball and paddle tennis in the streets all day and hanging around bowling alleys half the night. Her father had her put on boxing gloves and they'd spar and he'd sock her with his fists. He used to beat her with his belt too, if she upset him by coming home late or playing hookey from school.

She hated school, going mostly for the sports offered. She stole sidewalk fruit and once rented a bicycle, wheeled it around the corner, sold it for a fraction of its worth and used the money to go to Coney Island in a taxi. Sometimes she'd visit her aunt and uncle in Harlem. Her uncle made moonshine whisky and she'd drink it and when she, a mere child, arrived home drunk her father would beat her with a belt or—alternately—jam his fingers into her throat to make her sick to her stomach. There were times when she'd be afraid to go home so she'd climb aboard a subway car and sleep there.

In spite of her squalid surroundings, Althea Gibson climbed past every obstacle and became the first black player to dominate international tennis. That was in 1957, the year she turned thirty and broke through at both Wimbledon and Forest Hills. A year later, old as athletes are at thirty-one, she repeated in these world class events. Also, she won Wimbledon's doubles with Angela Buxton in 1957 and with Maria Bueno in 1958.

Yet none of these triumphs came as a surprise because as early as 1950, at twenty-three, Gibson made an indelible debut at Forest Hills: the first black ever to play in the national championships. She was well on her way to a second-round win over the Wimbledon champion, third-seeded Louise Brough, when rain stopped the match overnight. With so much time to think about an upset she was a nervous wreck the following morning. Brough capitalized on that, but the public had been made aware of a new dark threat.

It took time for Althea to fulfill her promise, though—a full seven years during which she kept fading in top tournaments. In June 1951, the first black to compete at Wimbledon, she lost to Beverly Baker in the quarter-finals. Later that year in the national indoors championships in Chicago she was bounced by Nancy Chaffee. In 1953 Mo Connolly beat her at Forest Hills and in 1954 Helen Perez dropped her in the first round there. By then Gibson's national ranking had dropped from seventh in 1953 to twelfth.

But in 1955 her career turned when she was named one of four American players to be sent on a good-will tour of Asia sponsored by the State Department. She won the Indian national and Asiatic women's singles championships. By the summer season of 1956 she was a tough player to bring down. She won both the Italian and French titles that spring.

In May 1957 when she left for Wimbledon from New York's Idlewild Airport only three people were there to wish her luck. When she returned with the Wimbledon championship the place was packed with scores who suddenly remembered how they'd helped Althea Gibson's career and now climbed on her bandwagon. The city fathers were delighted to have a home-town girl to shower ticker-tape on, too, a city eager to hear of her conversation at Wimbledon's Centre Court with Queen Elizabeth (the Queen had said, "It was a very enjoyable match, but you must have been very hot on the court." And Althea had replied, "I hope it wasn't as hot in the royal box.")

Everywhere that summer people wanted to hear from the black tradition-breaker. During a luncheon given for her by the city's mayor Robert Wagner at the Waldorf-Astoria Hotel, Althea was called upon to make a speech. "God grant that I wear this crown I have won with dignity," she said. "I just can't describe the joy in my heart." But she was realistic too. "Whenever I hear anyone call me 'Champ' I think there's something behind it," she said of the newly emerging well-wishers.

Gibson is remembered as a New Yorker who climbed a rough-and-tumble route from shouted arguments in Harlem to conversations with royalty and political luminaries. She was a product of New York's black ghetto, all right, although she was born on a farm in South Carolina on the outskirts of a little place called Silver. Her father Daniel thought the family of five (Althea was the oldest) would do better in the north than on the cotton-poor farm. He had five acres of land but foul weather ruined the crops three years in a row. "I worked three years for nuthin'," Althea remembers her father saying once. "That third year all I got out of it was a bale and a half of cotton. I made seventy-five dollars for the year's work."

So the Gibsons went north and settled in a house on Manhattan's swarming 143rd Street, and Daniel went to work in a garage. Kids played paddle tennis and shuffleboard on the baking streets in summer, supervised by a worker from the Police Athletic League.

Althea was a chronic truant at Public School 136, rushing off to play softball in Central Park or basketball at the 134th Street Boys Club with a team called the Mysterious Five. "I just wanted to play, play, play," she remembered in later years. "My mother would send me out with money for bread and I'd be out from morning to dark and not bring home the bread."

By 1940 when Althea turned thirteen the P.A.L. instructor, an unemployed musician named Buddy Walker, was impressed by the ferocious untrained skill of this young girl playing paddle tennis. He took her to a tennis-buff friend, Van Houton, a self-employed racquet stringer, who gave her a couple of second-hand racquets and directed her to hammer tennis balls against a wall of a handball court. When her consistency with ground strokes improved he took her to a one-armed professional named Fred Johnson at the Cosmopolitan Tennis Club, a virtually unique club where doors were open to blacks and whites alike.

Johnson taught Althea court tactics to augment the power of her game. Though only thirteen, the gangling youngster left school and took various jobs. She was a counter girl at a Chock Full o' Nuts shop in lower Manhattan at the opposite end of the island from Harlem, a long, long subway ride. Then she got a job cleaning chickens on Long Island, then one as an elevator operator in the Dixie Hotel in midtown, a packer in a button factory, and even as a mechanic in a machine shop where she tightened screws in sheets of metal.

Spare moments were filled with tennis. She entered and won her first tournament in 1942, the girls' championship of the Negro American Tennis Association's state championships in New York. Later that summer she went to the ATA's national tournament semifinals. One day on a crowded street in Harlem she recognized the popular boxing champion Sugar Ray Robinson. She pushed her way toward him and said defiantly, "You're Sugar Ray?

Well, I can beat you." Robinson laughed, amused by the arrogance of the lanky youngster almost as tall as he. (Althea eventually settled just under five feet eleven; her best playing weight was 145 pounds.)

At any rate, after considerable bantering with the not-quite-fifteen-year-old, Robinson invited her to go with him to meet his wife, Edna Mae. "She was very unhappy," Edna Mae remembered once. "She had a gaunt build and felt she was the least good-looking girl she knew. She had insecurity and went into herself. She used to talk wild. I tried to make her feel she could be something."

But segregation was blunting the ambition of the youngster. She dominated tennis among young black players—there were few opponents in a game belonging to private clubs that excluded blacks—so she hung around pool rooms, spent hours listening to jazz records in music stores or at the Robinsons, and blowing on a $150 saxophone Sugar Ray bought for her.

In 1946 when she turned nineteen Althea was old enough to play in the women's division of the Negro ATA's national championships. She got to the finals and lost, but her play attracted the attention of two ATA officials, Dr. Robert Johnson, a general practitioner from Lynchburg, Virginia, and Dr. Hubert Eaton, a surgeon from Wilmington, North Carolina. Dr. Johnson posed a question: "How'd you like to play at Forest Hills some day?" Althea didn't know if he was serious and she could see no humor. "Don't kid with me," she said flatly.

Johnson wasn't kidding. He and Eaton had been sufficiently impressed by the gangling, fiery, determined kid on the courts to give her an opportunity to reach her potential. With her family's blessing Althea was taken to the

Eaton home in Wilmington for the winter. She was sent to high school while Eaton and his wife worked on the development of her manners and her tennis game.

Dr. Eaton once recalled the picture Althea presented when she got off the train upon arriving in Wilmington. "There she was with Sugar Ray's saxophone in one hand and in the other an old pasteboard suitcase with two belts tied around it. She was wearing an old skirt—she'd apparently never owned a dress. My wife bought her a few dresses and tried to make her more feminine by getting her straight hair curled and showing her how to use lipstick."

Althea was not a compliant guest. She headed for a pool room where she felt comfortable, retreating there in embarrassment, perhaps, because her table deportment was so bad at the Eaton home they made her eat in the kitchen until it improved.

And at first, although nineteen, she couldn't qualify for the freshman class in high school. Yet she was bright, and by applying herself to her books she soon caught the swing of studies and moved right along.

Of course, the object of the Pygmalion exercise was to turn this raw youngster into a tennis player—of world class, if she had that in her—and to that end Eaton drilled her in fundamentals five or six times a week before school and after it. "I tried to show her how to be a lady on the court too," he said later, "but it was almost impossible for her to accept defeat with any kind of grace. If I ran up a 4–1 lead, say, she'd just quit. Anyone who could get a decent lead on her could beat her."

Althea went to Lynchberg in the vacation months and spent the summer taking tennis instruction from Dr.

Johnson. She also practiced with a robot machine that fired tennis balls across a net in a steady stream. She played in nine tournaments that summer of 1947 and won the singles title in every one. She and Johnson won eight mixed events too.

One of Gibson's singles victories was the ATA national championship, establishing her as the best black woman player anywhere. As it turned out, it was the first of ten consecutive triumphs—until she stopped playing in the tournament in 1957.

With her second ATA win in 1948 Althea provided fuel for the acceptance of blacks in the eastern grass-courts tournaments, posh events at fashionable summer spas. Jackie Robinson had been playing baseball for the Brooklyn Dodgers for two seasons, other blacks were headed for the big leagues, and large-scale social change appeared in the making. The ATA was advised that if Althea sent an entry to the Eastern Indoor Champion-ships in New York she'd be accepted. She did and she was and she lasted until the quarterfinals.

Meantime, she finished her high-school courses in three years and was graduated in June 1949, tenth in her class. She was offered a college scholarship by Florida A. & M., a school for black students in Tallahassee, which provided her with a room in the women's dormitory, books and tuition, and a job as assistant to the head of the women's physical-education department at forty dollars a month. She was twenty-two when she set foot in the school and considerably older than other freshmen, and twenty-five when she graduated. "I always thought of my-self as sort of aunt to the other kids," she once said.

Tennis, of course, was what took her there and tennis

was what she pursued. After winning her third ATA crown she went back to the national indoor tournament in New York and this time reached the final. She lost to Nancy Chaffee but when she stepped off the train at Tallahassee the gang at Florida A. & M. greeted her as though she'd just won Forest Hills.

Having done so well Althea felt she'd sprout wings if she could go opposite the top players at Forest Hills. But she couldn't get there until she'd qualified at one of the eastern grass tournaments along the Atlantic seaboard. No invitation was forthcoming from those exclusive tournaments-cum-social events and the USLTA acted as though she didn't exist or had never won anything.

Newspaper columnists began raising the point that there was no way for Gibson to play on the grass of Forest Hills in September if she couldn't play on it all summer, but no one at Seabright, East Hampton, Newport, Orange, Essex or the other grassy spas was reading. Or, anyway, heeding.

Then in the July 1950 issue of *American Lawn Tennis* magazine, former national champion Alice Marble attacked the hypocrisy of the American system. "Miss Gibson is over a cunningly wrought barrel, and I can only hope to loosen a few staves," Marble wrote. "I think it's time we faced a few facts. If tennis is a game for ladies and gentlemen, it's time we acted a little more like gentlepeople and less like sanctimonious hypocrites. If there is anything left in the name of sportsmanship, it's more than time to display what it means to us."

There was reaction but not much action. New Jersey's Maplewood Country Club refused to let Gibson on the courts for the state championship. However, South

Orange invited her to the Eastern Grass Courts championships. She lost in the second round but, having played in a grass event leading to the nationals, she could now play in them. Whereupon Sarah Palfrey took her under her wing. Sarah Palfrey was one of America's foremost players from 1930 to the mid-1940s, a notable doubles player who partnered Alice Marble to the Wimbledon title in 1938 and 1939 and won the U.S. doubles crown with lots of partners lots of times—Betty Nuthall, Helen Jacobs three times, Alice Marble four times and Margaret Osborne for a total of nine between 1930 and 1941. She was the national singles champion in 1941 and again in 1945.

Anyway, recognizing that Althea needed familiarization with Forest Hills's surroundings, Sarah arranged with the president of the West Side Tennis Club for practice periods for her and Althea on the famous grass (since deceased). It was a gesture that helped Gibson's game considerably and her head immeasurably. For one thing, she felt less lonely; she figured she had a friend in the blonde charmer Palfrey.

During the tournament she stayed with a longtime family acquaintance, Mrs. Rhoda Smith, on 154th Street in Harlem. To get to Forest Hills they walked four blocks to the Sixth Avenue subway station carrying Althea's tennis equipment, took a D train to 59th Street, changed to an F train there to cross from Manhattan to Forest Hills and got off at 71st Street and Continental Avenue, a three-block walk from the club entrance.

"I couldn't help but think that it had taken me a long time to make the trip," Althea reflected once. In more ways than one.

On the courts she skipped past Barbara Knapp of England in her first-round match, advancing a niche to meet Louise Brough, the Wimbledon champion who was seeded third at Forest Hills in a demonstration of chauvinistic oafism. Gibson was nervous and unable to concentrate in the first set and Brough ran it out quickly at 6–1. A heckler in the stands, displeased that a black should tread upon the sacred lawn, kept shouting to Brough, "Knock her out of there! Knock her out of there!" Still, Gibson settled down in the second set, handled Brough's best shots, and won the set 6–3.

"I built up a 7–6 lead in the third set and was feeling real good about my chances," Gibson recalled later. Then the courts were struck by a thunderstorm so violent they had to suspend play until the next day. "The delay was the worst thing that could have happened to me," Gibson said. "It gave me a whole evening and the next morning, too, to think about the match. By the time I got through reading the morning newspapers I was a nervous wreck."

Brough tied the match at 7–7 when they got on the court again, and then they struggled through an eighteen-point game on Gibson's serve before Brough forged ahead by 8–7 and jumped quickly into a 40–15 lead as she served for the match.

"I saved it once with a lob that Louise hit out," Gibson wrote, "but on her second try she made it. I hit a hard backhand that just went out, and Louise had won 6–1, 3–6, 9–7. Believe me, it was a long ride back to Harlem on the subway that afternoon."

Before she returned to school in Tallahassee she was advised by Hollis Dann of the USLTA that there'd be no objection from the association if she sent an entry to

Wimbledon the following summer but that she shouldn't entertain notions of financial help. The ruling fathers did arrange, however, for her to take instruction at Detroit from Jean Hoxie, a top-flight tennis teacher.

So in May, after she wrote final exams at Florida A. & M., Althea flew to Detroit for the lessons. She went to the Gotham Hotel where the manager told her Joe Louis had left word she was to use his personal suite. And on top of that Joe bought her a round-trip plane ticket to England so she could compete at Wimbledon.

All she really got there, though, was experience, followed by a disappointing season back home in the States. "I didn't advance as fast as a lot of people thought I should," Gibson reflected. "Maybe it was because I didn't get enough opportunities to play against topflight people." Whatever the reason, the years 1951, 1952 and 1953 were mostly disappointing. She was growing bored and restless and her national ranking dropped to No. 12 in 1954 and all that kept her interested in tennis was a job she got in the physical education department at Lincoln University in Jefferson City, Missouri, a school for black students where she taught for two years and coached the men's tennis team.

One afternoon in the summer of 1956 Althea learned that the State Department wanted her to tour Southeast Asia in a troupe that included a vivacious blonde named Karol Fageros, a Rhodes Scholar Ham Richardson, and a Californian Bob Perry.

The foursome's personalities meshed neatly and the tour took them to India, Pakistan, Thailand and Burma, where their task was to make friends for the U.S. and, of course, to endeavor to demonstrate the democracy of

America with this inclusion of a black in the contingent. When reporters raised questions of race problems Gibson had answers. "Sure, we have a problem in the States," she'd say. "All countries have problems of some sort. But it's a problem that's solving itself, I believe."

The tour ended in Ceylon in mid-January 1956. However, other countries had invited Althea to visit them. She served her cannonball in Cologne, in Lyon, in Cairo and in Alexandria. Altogether, she won sixteen out of eighteen tournaments playing from Rangoon to London. In Paris, she became the first black to win the French championships and in Rome the first black to win the Italian. And what she wanted next was to become the first black to win Wimbledon. She might have wanted it a little too much that summer of 1956 because when she came up against Shirley Fry in the quarterfinals she was far off her form, no match for Fry at all, really. Fry went on to win the championship.

She was Gibson's nemesis all summer: She beat her in the National Clay Court championships at Chicago and then in the nationals at Forest Hills where Gibson went to the final without dropping a set but where, in the final, Fry's calm and unruffled baseline game was the undoing of bounding hard-swinging Althea whose volleying did her in. The only sets she dropped in the tournament were two to Fry, 6–3 and 6–4, in the final.

In the wake of Forest Hills, Gibson began to work on her game steadily with a black pro from New York, Sydney Lewellyn, who regarded tennis as a geometric study, reasoning that for every shot there is one proper angle to answer it. Opponents meant nothing; only angles. He changed her grip too, which probably helped her game more than the angles. The switch gave her more fluidity in her volleying. She also picked up confidence—an absolute necessity.

She won the Pacific Southwest at Los Angeles, beating old rival Nancy Chaffee in the final. Then she toppled Darlene Hard in the Pan American final in Mexico City. She flew to Australia for the summer season that launched the new year Down Under, won the New South Wales and the South Australia championships and lost the Australian national final to—who else?—Shirley Fry.

"There was no getting away from it," she wrote later, reviewing her year. "Shirley had won all the big ones and I had won most of the little ones. I've got to make 1957 Althea Gibson's year."

So in May she embarked for London with three people waving farewell at Idlewild: her coach Sydney Llewellyn, her old friend Buddy Walker, and Edna Mae Robinson. Althea won three tournaments leading to the Wimbledon fortnight—Surbiton, Manchester and Heckenham—and in the big event itself she rushed through to the final round without dropping a set. With Queen Elizabeth in attendance in the royal box back of the baseline, the final was played on a most untypical English afternoon—the temperature flirting with 96 degrees and no breeze at all. But Gibson revelled in the heat, something that couldn't be said for her Californian opponent, Darlene Hard. Althea raced through the match in less than an hour, winning by 6–3 and 6–2.

"When I had won," she wrote in her memoirs, "they tell me I kept saying, 'At last! At last!' All I can remember doing is running to the net and shaking hands with Darlene and saying that she had played very well and that I had been lucky." The babbled cliches showed how much victory had meant to her; there was nothing lucky about her game and Hard had not been allowed to play well. Althea was clearly the better player and Hard could only stand well back when the Queen presented Gibson with a gold salver on which the names of all previous Wimbledon women's singles champions were engraved.

That night Althea Gibson dressed in a floor-length gown and went to the Wimbledon Ball in the Dorchester. She was escorted to the head table and seated between the Duke of Kent and the men's singles winner, Australian Lew Hoad. After dinner she asked the orchestra to play "April Showers" and she and Hoad danced the first dance, and Ham Richardson and Vic Seixas insisted she sing a couple of songs, and she sang "If I Loved You" and "Around the World", and it was the most wonderful night of high moments in the life of the one-time Harlem tomboy who became the queen of an elegant ball in one of London's storied hotels.

Other wonderful moments followed—the ticker-tape parade up Broadway to City Hall in New York and the luncheon at the Waldorf—and all through that summer and the next there were the victories on the tennis courts. She won the National Clay Courts crown at Chicago and romped through the rounds leading to the final at Forest Hills where her opponent turned out to be, fittingly enough, the woman she'd played there seven years earlier when she was breaking through—Louise Brough. Brough played fairly well in spots but, as Gibson wrote later, "she no longer was the player who had outlasted me back in 1950." Gibson, by no means the same player, either, won without difficulty 6–3 and 6–2.

She went back to England in 1958, carrying her serve-and-volley game to Centre Court with more confidence and power than she'd had a year earlier, and she had only one difficult match, a quarterfinal with Britain's Shirley Bloomer. She dropped the second set 8–6 after handily taking the opener 6–3. She was put down in the first two games in the final set and then finished Bloomer in six straight games. Ann Haydon Jones presented less difficulty in the semifinal, falling by 6–2 and 6–0, and Angela Mortimer was troublesome only in the opening set of the final as Althea won her second Wimbledon championship by 8–6, 6–2. The problem in the first set centered on a service technicality—foot faults were called on her nine times.

Forest Hills was scarcely more difficult than Wimbledon had been, though Darlene Hard started resolutely in the final and took the opening set at 6–3. But that was her only ripple. Gibson rushed through the next two sets with loss of three games.

Now she hoped to turn her amateur eminence into professional rewards. She received $100,000 from Abe Saperstein to travel with his Harlem Globe Trotters basketball madmen, playing exhibition matches between halves, but apart from that there wasn't money in the pros in the late 1950s. So Althea turned to professional golf. She was pretty good at it—for a tennis player—and made a steady if not gaudy living from it until the mid-1970s when in November 1975 she was appointed State Athletic Commissioner for New Jersey. She also became a partner in a sports equipment corporation in Newark. Then she resigned as athletic commissioner and dipped into politics, running for the New Jersey state senate.

When money began to fall on women's tennis, and Billie Jean and Chrissie and Evonne grew rich, Althea Gibson never lamented the timing on her own climb to the pinnacle, a relatively impecunious one. "When I think of where I started," she smiled on her fiftieth birthday in August 1977, "I feel I accomplished a great deal."

# VIRGINIA WADE

## [1945–   ]

Nine days away from her thirty-second birthday, Virginia Wade at long last won the women's singles championship at Wimbledon on the first day of July 1977 just when it seemed she was destined to become the most famous loser in the tournament's long history. As an emotional Briton appearing in her first final at the celebrated tennis shrine, she finally became the champion in her sixteenth attempt.

It was the year Queen Elizabeth celebrated her silver anniversary as monarch and the year Wimbledon celebrated its hundredth anniversary—the cen-*teen*-ery, the English called it. As any number of tennis historians recorded over that long span, no place name in the sphere of sports is quite so evocative as Wimbledon's.

It's a word that illuminates for people all over the world a fond remembrance of any number of sights and sounds. Such as, oh, the eight-mile tube ride from Charing Cross to the Southfields station in southwest London where an endless line of black taxis is parked on Wimbledon Park Road adjacent to the station, each waiting for five passengers to load quickly for the half-mile spin to the fifteen grass courts of the All-England Tennis Club in

*Virginia Wade*

the London suburb of Wimbledon with its population of sixty thousand.

Physically, the tennis club is a ten-acre cocoon where courts not bordered by grandstands are separated by paved walkways packed with people during the Wimbledon fortnight. Across the grounds up to thirty-five thousand tennis fans soak in the unhurried, polite, gentle atmosphere of ivy-draped walls and flower boxes and awnings and flat plates of strawberries with thick cream and the unique sound of a tightly strung racquet meeting a fuzzy yellow ball and the ohs and ahs of the mannered crowd when the points are ended.

"During the fortnight of the championships," Herbert Warren Wind wrote in the *New Yorker* about the Centenary, "when you walk around the grounds at Wimbledon—the Centre Court, surrounded by a dark-green twelve-sided structure, has seats for ten thousand six hundred and fifty-one people and standing room for about thirty-five hundred; the No. 1 Court has seats for fifty-five hundred and standing room for fourteen hundred; and there are fourteen other grass courts, three of which have fairly large stands—it strikes you as almost too impressive to be true."

All right. Anyone who has ever knocked an overhead smash fifteen feet beyond the baseline becomes helpless and dewy-eyed upon encountering this tradition-steeped tennis shrine. So for an English-born player the emotion is damned nearly unbearable—the stands at Centre Court alive with fourteen thousand spectators, most of them British and flag-waving and God-Save-the-Queen-singing, and the Queen herself sitting there in the royal box behind the baseline and flanked and backed by dukes and

FAMOUS WOMEN TENNIS PLAYERS

duchesses and princesses and princes and all manner of attendants, well, it's understandable that any Brit can scarcely jolly well *stand* the excitement and pressure and pomp and tradition, never mind the opposition across the net of the world's best tennis players.

Virginia Wade is not just *any* Brit. For many of the fifteen previous Wimbledons she had the style and form and intensity and class to bring off the women's championship, and for fifteen previous championships she'd blown it, one way or another, failing so often in her hollow-cheeked and stricken-faced and sweaty and leanly muscled and *furious* way to bang a winning shot in a key situation.

Often she'd make a big run, and draw front-page headlines two inches high. Over those sixteen tournaments she reached the quarterfinals seven times, went on to the semifinals twice, and on to the final this one time in 1977. And in the headlines she was always Ginny or Our Ginny or Poor Ginny as in GINNY FALLS IN SHOCK DEFEAT or OUR GINNY OUT! and POOR GINNY, YOU'VE GONE!

Hardly anyone expected her to make her sixteenth Wimbledon different, particularly since it was the cen*teen*-ery with all the added pressure of so special an occasion. She was seeded No. 3, a longshot at odds of sixteen to one in the legal betting shops where she was regarded one notch lower, fourth best. Chris Evert was the four-to-five favorite, Martina Navratilova, the bouncing Czech who was seeded No. 2, was five to one, and even the No. 5 seed, Billie Jean King, was more highly regarded by the bookies than OUR GINNY at six to one. Wade's sixteen to one left her far out of it.

But Virginia, who had gone to special pains in preparing for this Wimbledon, for once in her life did not fold; she especially did not fold after handling two of her most difficult longtime rivals, Rosie Casals in the quarterfinals and the indomitable (well, almost) Evert in the semis.

Her final-round opponent was the giant from Holland, wry and witty Betty Stove, who can on occasion make the finest shots in women's tennis and on occasion the absolute worst and who can intermingle them as though weaving a multicolored rug. Big Betty's game is what you call spotty. When she is good she is very very good and so on. Her concentration is her greatest asset but when she lets it wander, everything goes awry and the strong right arm on her six-foot-one frame goes slightly out of synchronization.

Wade took a great deal of psychological stress to the match—so near, so *near*—and chances are that a less determined player would have caved under the burden. But the thousands assembled saw a new Virginia Wade this day, new from her stylish short, fluffy Vidal Sassoon hairdo to a quite positive mental approach. Once nervous and uncertain, she felt this time, she said afterwards, that she was the strongest-willed person in the women's dressing room all through the tournament—one who had dreamed since she was a little girl of playing before the Queen, of holding high the gold plate of victory, and of winning the honor of opening the 1978 tournament on Centre Court as the defending champion, a traditional practice.

On the morning of the match she thought she might hide from distractions in her London flat just off Eaton

Square by placing a pillow over the telephone to absorb its ring. She put a symphony, Rachmaninoff's Second, at full volume on her record player to make sure that if the telephone did ring she wouldn't hear it.

But the doorbell rang instead, loud and insistent, and a band of press photographers wanted to shoot pictures of her on the morning of the great day.

"My first reaction was to tell them to clear off," she told assembled newshounds later. "I've played this Wimbledon differently to all the others and haven't even looked little children in the eye in case they want to distract me with autographs. But then I thought, 'What am I doing? Why be so prickly today of all days?' So I let them come in."

Then she went to the stadium early and walked into the silent Centre Court where not even the net or the net-posts were in place, just the flat expanse of grass worn yellow in patches by two weeks of play. She sat in the stands and her hazel eyes swept the dark green seats surrounding the solitary court.

"I feel it is absolutely necessary to go out onto the Centre Court before the match begins in order to get the atmosphere and to familiarize yourself with the court," she said afterwards. "So many times I have walked through that door onto the court and felt that I was walking into the most unfamiliar place in the world."

The Queen arrived at six minutes to two on this sunny afternoon when the stands were filled to the last dark-green corner with the expectant thousands. A military band at one corner of the court had just finished its rendition of "Land of Hope and Glory" when she took her place in the royal box. She was wearing a pink and white ensemble with an off-the-face turban, and with her were her husband, Prince Philip, the Duke of Edinburgh, and other members of the royal ensemble, Princess Margaret and the Duke and Duchess of Kent and their retinues, the attractive and matronly Duchess heavy with child. And seated back of this array of gentry were four British former winners of the Wimbledon singles title—Kitty Godfree (1924 and 1926), Dorothy Round (1934 and 1937), Angela Mortimer (1961) and Ann Haydon Jones (1969). The band struck up "God Save the Queen," and halfway through the fourteen thousand began to sing it softly.

Then the two finalists emerged from the dressing room beneath the draped royal box, turned to make curtsies, and then proceeded to warm up, hammering the new yellow balls with ground strokes and volleys and overhead smashes and services and finally, at a minute past two, the first ball was tossed, Wade serving.

It wasn't an easy match for the sentimental favorite to get into. Her Holland rival sportingly accepted the outrageous bias of the crowd but she declined to allow Wade to walk across her to get the title. The first game lasted five nervous minutes and soon it seemed the old Wade had returned, that the new one must still be savoring her win of two days previous over Chris Evert.

But there was one vital difference this time. Wade wasn't allowing her mistakes to upset her. Even so, she hit her worst spell in the ninth game when she lost her own serve at love; and when Big Betty held hers she had the first set.

But Virginia came back. Prowling the court, exhorting herself, slapping her thigh with her right hand when things didn't go well, scowling, grimacing, she won the first game of the second set and then got a gift from Stove when the curly headed Hollander, fidgeting between serves with an elastic support that braced her left knee, double-faulted twice in the second game. Wade quickly made it 3–0 with her own service and seemed well on her way.

But nothing is ever that simple with Virginia. She promptly lost the next three games, and the highly emotional throng doing all sorts of wishful thinking and, indeed, contributing everything short of audible prayers toward victory, now brought forth a prolonged groan. There were signs she was beginning to tense up. But, wait, not this time. As one player said of Wade:

"The old Ginny would have gone on until the blood vessels were sticking out on her forehead, and she would have blown four games in the meantime. The new Virginia went and sat on the grass by the umpire's chair and relaxed her neck and back muscles. She sees the signs now. It's the same car but it's being driven by a different person."

Unquestionably, this was the match's decisive moment—the first set gone, the 3–0 lead vanished, the heat definitely on and Big Betty cruising stoically. But Wade survived it, and men's eyes glazed: "Miss Wade had all the crashing, pounding fury of a mountain stream following a well-defined course as she held her service for 4–3," is how the gentleman from the London *Times,* Rex Bellamy, described it next day. "That mighty if discreet show of authority swung the match irrevocably from the Netherlands to Britain. Miss Wade won seven consecutive games. Her burning intensity of will was becoming evident in sudden private gestures. She was whipping herself along: 'Keep going. Watch the ball.' Miss Stove was done for."

And then the second set was over and, soon, so was the third with the loss of only a single game, and what a roar there was, what a happy sea of hands. And the Queen went down from the royal box and flags waved everywhere and there was a spontaneous chorus of "For She's a Jolly Good Fellow" and no one quite knew if the voices were raised for the queen of the realm or the queen of tennis. Big Betty tried to cruise quietly from view and let the Brits have their moment alone, as it were, but Prince Philip moved across the scuffed turf to take her arm and guide her back to the festivities.

When the relaxed and jovial Stove faced the press in an airless concrete tomb in the bowels of the grandstand she said she'd tried to stay calm and to keep the pressure on Wade in that second-set turning point. "But Virginia started to serve better," she reconstructed. "She began coming to the net more. There was more pressure on me because she was more relaxed than ever before. She has matured. She has learned. You should give her credit for that. How do I feel? Me? Oh, you know, fine, great, okay."

And when Virginia spoke, she talked of her new approach to tennis, the new philosophy, the rearranged game. She had gone to Los Angeles to a professional there, sixty-year-old Jerry Teeguarden, and he had helped her realign her forehand and her service, normally one of the finest instruments of women's tennis but one that had soured.

She was glowingly pleased to have won the biggest prize on her home turf after so many years. "The result means everything to me," she said in that tiny vault of a room, her face lean and drawn yet *alive*. "Everyone thought I was past it and couldn't do it. I have worked so incredibly hard for this tournament. I think I have really been rather brave. I got Mr. Teeguarden to help me and completely change parts of my game. It takes a lot of courage to alter your game and not to be disappointed when you don't get results to start with."

She tried earnestly to convey her feelings, to give a sense of what she felt to journalists from the big national dailies and from Italy and France and Canada and the United States and other countries where the game is popular and Wade's spunk and skill and emotionalism are admired.

"I wanted to prove I deserved to be out there with all those champions. I felt I belonged, that I was the best player who hadn't won Wimbledon, and it was wonderful to win it in front of the Queen, but the cheering was so loud it was difficult to hear what she said to me. All I heard her say was 'Well played. It must have been hard work.' I told her that it *was* hard work but that I had more incentive this week than I ever had before."

She talked of the way players reacted to one another in the dressing room. "I've definitely changed my attitude there in the past couple of years. You can always tell the people who are at ease with themselves. I just felt this week that I was by far the strongest person in the dressing room. I felt I had more guts and was more secure than anyone else." She said she wasn't the least bit embarrassed by the partisan enthusiasm that surrounded Centre Court during her match with Betty Stove. "I felt it was my tournament and my match—and that I could have all that and not feel guilty about it."

Beating Chris Evert two days earlier was very close to being Virginia Wade's finest performance on a tennis court. Instead of being tentative in it or in any way cowed by Evert's towering record, the power of her ground strokes or the celebrated Centre Court jitters, Wade played an almost perfect match. Herb Wind noted that in the three sets Wade only twice hit a ground stroke that carried beyond the baseline, almost unheard-of control. "Miss Wade is often given to dithering and stumbling about when she is in sight of victory," Wind wrote. "We knew it really was a new Virginia after her semi-final with Chris Evert."

And the headlines in Saturday's national newspapers were marvellously British. BY GINNY, IT'S MINE! cried the *Daily Express* in two-inch capital letters on its front page, and TRUE GRIT OF GINNY on the back one. The *Daily Mail* squealed JUBILEE GINNY! on the front, GINNY—MY DREAM HAS COME TRUE on the back. The proper *Times* had a proper head on its lead story in the sports section: WIMBLEDON ACCLAIMS MISS WADE. Of course.

The British acclaim was tumultuous partly because the tournament was its very own, and was by no means an indication that Wimbledon was the first event the fiery brunette and favorite daughter had ever won in the upper echelons of tennis. Indeed, nine years earlier, just turned twenty-three, Wade had shown she belonged with world-class players by jarring Billie Jean King in straight sets in the final at Forest Hills.

Wade's first year of full-time tennis was 1967 and the national titles she won between then and Wimbledon ten years later, apart from the 1968 conquest at the United States national championships, included the Italian and the Australian singles, the French and Australian doubles in 1973 with Margaret Court, and the Italian doubles that same year with the young Russian Olga Morozova. She and countrywoman Ann Haydon Jones reached the Wimbledon semifinal in 1966 and 1967 when Wade was just getting underway.

But not long before that she had decided to devote less time to tennis and more to her studies. After she graduated from secondary school she entered Sussex University to specialize in mathematics and physics. She continued to play in tournaments but the combination was taking its toll academically and on the court too. Realizing she couldn't do justice to both, she settled into the scholastic part of her life.

Then in the middle of her final examinations in 1966 the tennis association pressured her into rejoining the Wightman Cup team for matches against the Americans at Wimbledon. Wade agreed, and took to dashing between the shrine of tennis and the hall of learning, writing exams on the one side and trying to handle the ground strokes of people like Nancy Richey on the other. The result was a close loss in tennis and third-class honors at school instead of either a hoped-for victory or second-class honors, whichever. So she turned to full-time tennis for an exploratory fling.

The game came naturally to Wade, the youngest of four children of Eustace Holland Wade, an Anglican clergyman, whose calling had settled him in Bournemouth, a resort town on England's south coast. The family was there in July 1945 when Sarah Virginia arrived on the scene, and she was a mere eleven months old when the Reverend Wade moved the family to South Africa, his wife's home country. Later, he served as archdeacon of Durban and canon of Natal. In Durban, by coincidence, the family lived next door to the Durban Lawn Tennis Club. All four Wade children were attracted to tennis, with Virginia getting instruction from her sister and two brothers when she was nine, innocently launching a career that turned her into a wealthy young woman before she was thirty. Obviously, she liked the game from the start: when her siblings were absent she spent hours pounding a tennis ball against the garden wall.

She never received intense fundamental instruction, only specific adjustments like those administered by Jerry Teeguarden prior to the 1977 Wimbledon. On another occasion, in 1965 in Cleveland, she was a girl of nineteen under the aegis of Maureen Connolly when Little Mo was brought in to coach the British Wightman Cup team. Connolly and her husband Norman Brinker established a tennis foundation in Dallas, and later on Wade and Ann Jones occasionally went there for rest, skilled instruction and friendly advice. Wade once said her respect for Connolly affected the development of her game and her determination to play it with a high technical gloss.

Indeed, more than one tennis buff has noted that with Wade the winning or losing of a tennis match sometimes is secondary to technique, and that her regard for the aesthetic side combined with her emotionalism and her unpredictability provide a dimension that's enormously attractive to fans.

Still, by the time the Wade family returned to England when Virginia was sixteen, tennis was by no means a consuming passion. "I played in tournaments because it was the thing to do and because I wanted a scrapbook," she was quoted by Galway Kinnell in *Sports Illustrated* in 1973. She was also interested in math and physics, which were her majors in university, and in music; she studied piano. And although Wightman Cup took her away from the sciences at Sussex, she did graduate with a Bachelor of Science degree.

One of her most impressive early wins was in the final of the Dewar Cup tournament at Stalybridge where she handled Ann Jones in straight sets in the final. The left-handed Jones, Britain's top player that summer, had gained the semifinals at Wimbledon along with Maria Bueno, Billie Jean King and Margaret Smith Court. There, she had lost to the fluid stylist from Brazil in the tournament's most emotional match by 6–3, 9–11, 7–5. In the Dewar Cup, then, few felt twenty-year-old Wade was ready for Jones. A year later she handled her again, this time in the British Hard Court championships at Virginia's birthplace, Bournemouth.

Now the ups and downs of Wade's career began to manifest themselves. She lost to an unknown Australian, Faye Moore, in the Italian singles final, then scored over Nancy Richey in her singles match in the Wightman Cup, and returned to Bournemouth for another hard-court title. So her public naturally began to hope that Britain was now developing a Wimbledon champion, which the country had been unable to do since Angela Mortimer's win in 1961, the only success in the entire post-World War II period.

But it was a case of OH, GINNY! A SHOCKER! for the headline writers in that 1967 Wimbledon. Virginia was unceremoniously axed in the first round by unseeded and unheralded Christina Sandberg. Her 1968 season, the first year of open tennis, was no less baffling. She was seeded sixth and an outsider at Forest Hills but, typically, moved resolutely through the lists, shading Rosie Casals, Ann Jones, and the Australian Judy Tegart who had been runner-up to Billie Jean by 9–7, 7–5 at Wimbledon that summer.

And now in the final at Forest Hills it was Billie Jean across the net from her, the bespectacled Californian who had beaten her eight times in nine meetings over the previous two summers. Wade was lightly regarded against the defending champion naturally, but in what was becoming characteristic she performed the unexpected with a 6–4, 6–2 win and became the first Briton to win the American championship since Betty Nuthall in 1930.

The British papers grew ponderous as well as glib over this victory. Along with OUR GINNY DOES IT! there was this from David Gray in the *Guardian:* "It was like watching a heavy gun blow down walls. It was as though Miss Wade had suddenly put together the jigsaw of her temperament and talent."

Famous last words. In 1969 Wade lost to people who

had never survived a first round at Wimbledon, people whose names were scarcely known to distant relatives. She lost to famous players too, such as Ann Jones at Monte Carlo in the Monaco Open and Billie Jean at Dublin in the Irish Open. In September she lost her United States Open title in the semifinal round to Margaret Court. So, with everybody beating her, naturally she throttled old rival Ann Jones in the Dewar Cup final.

If that win indicated Virginia was back on track, she dispelled the notion in 1970 when she didn't win a tournament, not even that old standby, the hard-court championship at Bournemouth.

But if that setback indicated Virginia was off track, she dispelled the notion in 1971 when she went to Rome and won her first Italian Open.

This inconsistency has been the subject of numerous dissertations. Some have put it down to Wade's inability to get her emotions under control when matches are important—such as Wimbledon—and others have blamed it on her pursuit of technical perfection on lesser occasions. Joanna Kilmartin interviewed Wade on the subject for the London *Observer* and came away with this from the temperamental star: "I've got an incredibly wide range of shots, which is also half the problem. You've got six different ideas to choose from and you end up hitting the ball into the net. In this way, intelligence is detrimental to tennis. I'd much rather lose than play ugly tennis on slow courts, and this is worrying because you should want to win at all costs."

And when Galway Kinnell was writing about her in *Sports Illustrated* he claimed Wade underwent her nerve-wracking inner struggle all through her matches. "Not until the last point is played can one know whether she will prevail or collapse."

By 1972 Wade was back at her peak again, beating Evonne Goolagong in straight sets in winning the Australian championship, capturing the Dewar Cup final again, and rushing through the early rounds at Wimbledon in both singles and doubles (with Rosie Casals) in splendid form.

CAN GINNY DO IT? the *Sun* wanted to know, and for a time it seemed the answer might have to be OUR GINNY DOES IT! The pressure kept mounting as she advanced through four rounds and, with Rosie, stroked onward and upward in the doubles. David Hunn, in the *Observer,* could scarcely stand the strain, finding her style to be "ruthless, beautiful and devastating" but too perfect to last. "Virginia Wade can't—or won't—keep this up," David warned. "But while she does there is no finer sight in tennis."

David knew. In the fifth round Virginia tangled once again with Billie Jean. She had jitters in the first set and lost it 6–1. She frequently brought the packed Centre Court gallery happily to its feet in the second set, giving hope with a 6–3 win. Then she subsided to Billie Jean's deep hard volleys and lancing backhand, 6–3.

Virginia returned to the yellowing grass later in the afternoon with Casals to win a Wimbledon championship at last. They beat Francoise Durr of France and Ann Jones 7–5 in the third set. The British association's tallest foreheads were so pleased they named Virginia captain of both their Wightman Cup and Federation Cup teams for 1973.

Wade started 1973 off with a smash. She encountered

the eighteen-year-old ice maiden from Florida, Chris Evert, in the semifinals of the Maureen Connolly Brinker tournament in Dallas and outlasted her, surprisingly, in the thirty-three-game marathon by 2–6, 6–3, 9–7. Then she went against the formidable Goolagong in the final in a meeting of a pair of unpredictables. Goolagong was as famous for her walkabouts, when she strolled the court daydreaming, as Wade for her inconsistency. This time, Wade was on top of her game, sweeping aside the lithe Aussie 6–4 and 6–1.

By the summer of 1974 World Team Tennis was a reality, a whole new concept in the pros in which a broad-based circuit in the U.S. and eastern Canada banded together in teams playing one-set matches—singles, doubles, mixed—with the scores of the games contributing to an overall total for a win or a loss in team standings. In June Wade was signed by the New York Sets, who later became the Apples, to play the second half of the first WTT season for $40,000.

With the Apples serving as an operating base, Wade took a New York apartment with her friend Mary Lou Mellace, whose philosophy that ambition can be achieved by guts and determination has been a great aid to Wade. That and the intensive instruction and practice with teammates Ray Ruffles, Sandy Mayer, Billie Jean and Fred Stolle on the Apples right through the 1977 season lifted her game to new dimensions. They'd practice three hours on non-match days and two hours before matches—sometimes two players against one, sometimes one on one, sometimes four at the net practically nose to nose banging volleys to sharpen reflexes.

Wade moved out from there to the big tournaments

when she wasn't heavily involved on the Virginia Slims women's circuit. She lost to her one-time doubles partner Olga Morozova in the Wimbledon semifinal in 1974, then to Goolagong in the same bracket there two years later.

And then at Wimbledon in 1977 everything came together for Sarah Virginia Wade and she established once and for all that she had the inner will and the outer skill to handle the suffocating pressure of the tournament that meant more to her than any championship anywhere. As the *Daily Mail* might say: OUR GINNY'S GOT IT!

*Evonne Goolagong*

# EVONNE GOOLAGONG

[1951-      ]

It's a cliché, of course, but in truth it's next to impossible to escape the notion Evonne Goolagong was born to play tennis. Look at it this way:

Here is the third of eight children—four boys and four girls—living in the middle of the Australian nowhere four hundred miles southwest of Sydney. The family knows nothing and cares nothing about tennis. The father makes a modest living as a sheep-shearer. A couple of battered old tennis balls find their way into the home only because the father happens to buy a second-hand truck that happens to have three old tennis balls lying forgotten under the seat.

The Goolagongs are the only Aboriginal family in the hamlet of Barellan, population nine hundred, where they eke out a living. Australians are as prejudiced as people anywhere, but the Goolagongs are accepted by neighbors because in a town so small nobody has any real need to kick somebody to feel important. Also, the Goolagongs live in a rundown house on the edge of town and so are no threat to anyone.

As a child Evonne was only interested in playing with a tennis ball, not in dolls or doll houses or cutouts, as her sisters were. "It was her constant companion," her mother told writer John Dunn in 1971. "She would hold it in her hand and squeeze it all day long. Later she would bounce it and catch it and hit it with a broomstick. She was never without it."

Remarkably, even before she started school she was earning money retrieving balls at the Barellan tennis club. When she got a racquet as a present at age six she spent days hitting tennis balls with it.

The president of the War Memorial Tennis Club in Barellan, watching the curly-haired child swing the racquet, began showing her the rudiments of stroking the ball. When she was ten the man, W. C. Kurtzman, put her name into a children's tournament at a nearby town and discovered upon arriving that the tournament was for adults. But since she was entered and since they were there, the child and the man remained at the courts and the child won all her matches and the tournament's top prize for women. And as a capper, if you still don't feel Evonne Goolagong was born to play tennis, a year after she left Australia for the first time, she won the ultimate tennis tournament, Wimbledon, and in the final two rounds defeated the two best women players in the world, Billie Jean King and Margaret Court, without loss of a set. She was nineteen.

But, really, it's not that she's a winner that sets Evonne Goolagong apart, it's *how* she wins—and, for that matter, how she loses. "She plays Wimbledon and the other big tournaments as though she were a kid playing in a meadow," Bud Collins, tennis writer and broadcaster, wrote once. "Her naturalness in beaming her humanity— the smile, the good-natured shrug, the tiny 'Oops, I've made a booboo' shriek, her obvious feeling that it's really only a game—wins love from an audience that deals out admiration to others."

In America, where winning is the only thing, Evonne Goolagong is a phenomenon. She apparently feels as well after a match she's lost as a match she's won, which of course is incomprehensible. She smiles, she laughs, she doesn't berate officials, she doesn't complain that the crowds are too noisy or the courts too bumpy or the weather too cold. If you think of everything you can possibly remember about the manners and attitude and behavior of Jimmy Connors and his boorish sidekick Ilie Nastase on a tennis court, those are what Evonne Goolagong is not.

And it is not some kind of act she has dreamed up. "What you see is what there is with Evonne," Rosie Casals said once. "Win or lose, the sun will come up tomorrow. She's as nice and pleasant as she seems, no brooding, no introspection. Who can be like that? Nobody else I've run into in this life."

The ingenuousness can be disconcerting. The man who raised her, guided her, developed her game, Australian coach Vic Edwards, said once there'd never be another player like her. He said it in exasperation. "I'm at a loss to explain what goes on in her head," he sighed. "Especially when she loses matches because her mind wanders off."

The fresh and unaffected Goolagong plays tennis with a brisk and buoyant sense of enjoyment, an enthusiastic serenity. She is gifted for the game, with a swift grace of balanced movement, an instinctive tactical brain, and a flexible bank of strokes. She can quickly assess the strengths and weaknesses of opponents, and her concentration is hilarious, with her renowned 'walkabouts.' "

"If there's not enough prodding from my opponent, if she's not challenging, well, the Goolagong fog descends and I vanish in a haze of inattention," are her words in her autobiography ghosted by Bud Collins in his customary glibness. "The Goolagong form is still out there, hacking away and losing points, but I'm on automatic pilot. When this happens, my fans groan 'not again,' my coach Mr. Edwards tries to light two cigarettes at once, muttering 'bloody' . . . something or other, and most spectators nod knowingly, 'Evonne's gone walkabout.' "

Once, in a match in Dusseldorf against Heidi Orth, Evonne dropped the first set and was headed for a second trimming in the next when suddenly she turned matters so completely around that Orth didn't win another game. Exasperated, Edwards wanted an explanation afterwards. "Well, uh, I was trying to think of this tune," she told him, "and it just wouldn't come to me. But then in the second set I got it, and started humming it, and everything was all right. Yes, I guess I was in a bit of a fog until then."

She was embarrassed once to come upon Chris Evert crying after a defeat. Evert had been shaded by Billie Jean in the first tournament Goolagong ever played in the U.S., the Maureen Connolly event in Dallas in 1972, knocking Chris out of the quarterfinals by 7–5 in the third set.

"I went into the locker room to change for a doubles match," she recalled, "and there was Chrissie bawling her eyes out. I never know what to say to someone who's taking a loss so hard. I can't understand it. I thought, 'I hope I never come to this.' I'll know something's wrong if I do. Games aren't something to cry over."

She was beaten in several she could have cried over. She was the finalist for four straight years without success in the U.S. nationals, 1973 through 1976, and survived psychologically—indeed, laughing. She lost thrilling matches to Margaret Court by 7–6, 5–7, 6–2 in the 1973 final, to Billie Jean by 3–6, 6–3, 7–5 the next year and to Evert 5–7, 6–4, 6–2 the year after that. In 1976 Chris hammered her 6–3, 6–0 in the only one-sided affair. Typical of her reaction to these setbacks was her remark to Collins after the loss to Billie Jean. "It will probably take me until tomorrow to forget it," she told him, apparently in all seriousness after confessing that the loss had cut deeper than most.

Of course she won far more matches than she lost—big matches. She took the Australian Open three times, 1974 and 1975 and then again in 1978 after she gave birth to her first child. Along with Wimbledon in 1971 she won the French Open in Paris. In 1972 she won the Canadian and the South African national championships and the U.S. National Indoor title, and a year later she repeated at Toronto and won the Italian Open in Rome. Indeed, by the time she turned twenty-two in 1973 she had won seventeen singles championships in thirteen nations.

Vic Edwards, a man whose long and valued guidance ended when Goolagong defied his strenuous insistence that she not marry Englishman Roger Cawley in June 1975, was almost entirely responsible for her development into a tennis champion. He took her into his Sydney home when she was thirteen and with his wife Eva raised her with their five daughters, practically a Henry Higgins working with a racquet-wielding Eliza Doolittle.

Whenever newsmen came upon them they found Edwards to be blunt, outspoken, occasionally rude and always straightforward, very sure that his way was the right way and the *only* way, a big drinker, heavy smoker, a man born in 1909 who dedicated a large piece of his life toward endeavoring to make Goolagong the world's best tennis player.

In 1970 when he took her on her first overseas tour he discouraged her dating, fearing she'd fall in love to the detriment of her game. But she met Cawley, a tennis buff who owned a printing business in London, and continued to see him over the objections of Edwards in visits to England. The rift reached its peak just before the 1976 Wimbledon tournament when she married Cawley.

She played a brilliant tournament that summer, then lost to Evert in a thrilling final, 6–3, 4–6, 8–6, her fourth final there in six years. A year later she was on hand for the Wimbledon Centenary but as a spectator. A month earlier she had given birth to a daughter, Kelly Inala.

Edwards made a great tennis player of her but nature gave her grace and fluidity of motion equalled since the days of Suzanne Lenglen herself only by Maria Bueno. She rarely made an awkward gesture or hit a ball off balance. "She doesn't seem conscious of her body at all," Julie Heldman once said. "It just works for her." Grace Lichtenstein, who wrote a book about the women's tennis revolution, found herself thinking of Willie Mays when she watched Goolagong—"the happy, not-so-bright jock who loved baseball so much he played stickball in the streets of Harlem after he had finished a game at the Polo Grounds."

Evonne acquired the mechanics from Edwards. "Repetition is the heart of learning tennis, hitting shots over and over until they become second nature, thousands and thousands of shots," it is recorded in her autobiography. The essence of the Edwards method she calls The Drill, a routine of component parts of a tennis stroke—ready-position stance, backswing, impact-making swing that creates either spin, slice or topspin, and follow-through. "You go through it again and again, without hitting a ball," her book says, noting that a photograph on the wall of Edwards' office shows his daughter Jenifer, at age nine, standing on a platform at White City Stadium in Sydney leading hundreds of children in The Drill.

Evonne was a five-year-old child in Barellan when Bill Kurtzman led a subscription drive to raise money for four red loam courts and the beginning of the War Memorial Tennis Club. It was Kurtzman who realized as the youngster grew older and her tennis skills continued to improve that she needed the sort of expert instruction she'd never find in Barellan. He talked to Edwards who was running his tennis school in Sydney, persuading him to give lessons to Evonne during her summer vacation when she was eleven, and he also arranged for her to board with the Edwards family for three weeks. By the time she was thirteen she was winning national attention as a tennis prodigy. When she won the under-fifteen championship of New South Wales people began to say she looked as promising as Margaret Smith had been at a similar age.

By this time Edwards was convinced she could reach the top rung in tennis, and he told Kurtzman as much.

"But there's only one way this can happen," Edwards said. "She must come and live with us full time, be part of our family." Edwards wasn't completely altruistic. "But,

Bill," he added, "what are you and the people of Barellan prepared to do, even if this is all right with Melinda and Ken Goolagong? Evonne's welcome in my home but I can't pay for her entire upkeep."

Kurtzman talked to the girl's parents, who loved their daughter but agreed to let her live in the Edwards home in Sydney. Evonne's mother, Melinda, was pregnant ten times, starting at age sixteen. "She lost two through miscarriages," Evonne noted once, "and she wouldn't mind having eight more children."

After Kurtzman talked to Edwards he canvassed the War Memorial club. He got pledges of six dollars a week from enough members to account for Evonne's keep with the Edwards family, so Evonne took off for Sydney.

"We left everything to Mr. Edwards," Kenneth Goolagong told writer John Dunn in 1971. "We still do. We know that whatever he decides will be in Evonne's best interest."

Edwards eventually became the youngster's legal guardian, and he and his wife brought her up with their five daughters. Evonne graduated from the Willoughby Girls' High School in Sydney, completed a speech course at Trining College, and like the Edwards brood got private instruction in elocution and deportment. Edwards had her take a secretarial course too, in case her tennis career failed to jell.

She often played tournament doubles with Patricia Edwards (Tricia, with whom she was closest in the family). At sixteen she won every Australian national junior title without losing a set. Between 1968 and 1970 she won forty-four singles and thirty-eight doubles championships as an Aussie amateur.

By 1970 Edwards figured she was ready for overseas experience, and lined up twenty-one European tournaments in Britain, France, Holland and Germany. She won seven, including the Welsh and Bavarian championships, even knocked over Rosie Casals in the third round of the British Hard Court Championships in Bournemouth. By the time she reached Wimbledon for the first time, practically everybody in tennis was ready for a look at the eighteen-year-old star.

"Here she was, trembling," Bud Collins wrote. "And here we were, curious and expectant. We'd read about her, heard about her, and now . . . now . . . ladies and gentlemen—the Great Dark Hope—Evonne Goolagong!"

The Boston blabbermouth was jesting, of course. Things weren't quite that agog. But he said later that Goolagong, full of nerves, showed enough in her match with American Peaches Bartkowicz to indicate she was definitely a comer. She was walloped 6–4, 6–0 by Bartkowicz—"a husky woman with a fierce stare and a two-fisted backhand," Evonne recalled once—awed by "all those faces, fourteen thousand people, about twenty-eight times the population of Barellan." The match had been put on Centre Court because of the glowing accounts of Goolagong's game preceding her arrival.

Edwards was philosophical about the blitzing. "In the second set the panic set in and all Evonne wanted was to get off the court," he recorded later. "This has happened to all-time greats; Evonne is no exception. At 4–5 she served three double faults to lose the set, then fell to pieces completely and didn't win another game. It is up to me to convince her that this year on the road is only for experience."

He was successful. Early in 1971 she shaded her childhood idol Margaret Court by 7–6, 7–6, displaying a quality that often eluded Court—the capacity to weather pressure. A *Sports Illustrated* report took this into account: "At no stage did she hesitate to go for winners, even when she was in the most desperate position. Time after time she appeared in a hopeless position but saved herself with tremendous backhand volleys or fine passing shots."

Edwards predicted Goolagong would win Wimbledon by 1974, but as early as 1971, a mere twelve months after her lesson from Peaches Bartkowicz, she returned there and played with the confidence of a champion. By then, she had experienced a great deal, for en route she became involved in a racial controversy in South Africa. Also, she went against some of the world's best players in the French championships at the testing Roland Garros Stadium in Paris.

Politically naive, a lamb in the ways of the world, Goolagong regarded the South African Open as she might a tournament in Barellan. By 1971 many athletes were distraught over the South African government's apartheid policy that discriminated unconscionably against the majority black population, and sports associations in soccer, cricket and rugby, games favored by the white population there, boycotted international competition in those sports when South Africans were involved with their all-white teams, the only kind they had.

In tennis, the promoter of the South African Open, Owen Williams, believed a chink in the government's policy of prejudice might be achieved if the Aboriginal Goolagong were to play tennis against pure-as-the-driven-snow whites in beautiful downtown Johannesburg. The young star's ghosted memoirs relate that she felt South Africa was just another name of another country where there was another tennis tournament.

"I couldn't believe the furor that erupted in Australia when it was announced that I'd been invited to visit that country and play in that tournament." Collins has her confessing to being "confused, troubled and even a little frightened" by the furor. Of course, she had nothing to do with whether she'd play in South Africa or not. It was Vic Edwards' decision and he decided they'd go.

The whites in South Africa treated her as though she were a human being as she played through to the final round where Margaret Court beat her. The prime minister of Australia, William McMahon, felt disposed to wire her his congratulations for being "a good ambassadress." She went back in 1972 and 1973, beating Virginia Wade the first time and losing to Chris Evert the next. Playing against the whites did not cause the sky to fall nor did it affect the South African government's policy of segregation.

At any rate, Goolagong moved on to the French Open and sped through the first six rounds without losing a set. She met pat-balling Frenchwoman Francoise Durr in the quarterfinals, was tied with her at 3–3 in the first set and then won nine straight games.

That put her against another unorthodox performer, Hollander Marijke Schaar. Schaar has *no* backhand. Being ambidextrous, she flips her racquet from hand to hand and hammers the ball with a forehand, no matter what. Evonne bounced merrily into the final against countrywoman Helen Gourlay at the expense of the forehanding Schaar, and though down love-three and 2–5 in

167

the second set and with five set points to overcome, she managed to prevail over Gourlay by 6–3 and 7–5.

Moving to Wimbledon, Goolagong was in line to meet Peaches Bartkowicz in the second round, but Peaches was pitted against Kristien Kemmer in the first and lost. Then Evonne made short work of Kemmer. In succession she put down Julie Heldman in straight sets, Lesley Hunt in three, and gained the semifinals against Billie Jean King by allowing Nancy Richey Gunter five games.

King quickly undertook her serve-and-volley game but Goolagong simply kept knocking passing shots crosscourt or down the line beyond Billie Jean's reach and won by 6–4, 6–4 in a close-to-flawless performance. Now she was in against Big Momma, Margaret Court, in the final.

In a most surprising way, considering her youth and the tension that usually settles upon Centre Court with all that atmosphere and all those faces and all that reverence and all those royals, Goolagong sped off to a 4–0 lead and the crowd ate her up like strawberries sunk in Devonshire cream.

Margaret kept plodding stoically and soon was whittling into the lead, bringing reality to the dreamy scene. She climbed to 3–4 and banged ahead 40–15 with Goolagong serving. This was a crisis point for Evonne; dropping her serve here would turn everything around, deadlocking the match. Still, she charged the net behind her first serve and put away a forehand volley for 30–40. Now her first serve missed; she got the second deep enough that Court wasn't able to pounce on it. After a short rally Court came in quickly and blasted a crosscourt forehand. Evonne just got to it, lifting a lob and laying the ball against the baseline with enough topspin to fling it past the hastily backtracking Margaret for deuce. It was a significant shot especially when two quick Court errors gave her game and a 5–3 lead instead of the 4–4 deadlock. When Court held service to cut that margin to 5–4 the shot's importance mounted higher. Now Evonne could win the set by holding her service.

With the crowd entreating for such an event, Goolagong gave them chills. Serving at 30-all she rushed forward, got a forehand opportunity—and knocked the ball into the net. At 30–40, she levelled it at deuce with a splendid overhead, then blew the first point there to provide Court with another break opportunity. Still rushing in, Evonne's volley hit the netcord. The ball somehow climbed the cord and fell on Court's court. Deuce again. Once more to the net and this time a forehand winner. Set point. To the net again. Court lifted a lob short and Evonne's smash won the set—finally.

Usually, tennis players regard the first game of the second set as pivotal, a way of establishing who's really in charge. Court got ahead 40–15 this time, but Evonne deuced it, and then there were three more deuces before Margaret iced the game with two big forehands.

A big psychological edge, right?

Wrong.

Goolagong won six straight games. Her overhead and her backhand were devastating. She seemed simply inspired. She got ahead 40–0 as Margaret served at 1–5 with three match points upcoming—and lost them all. The renowned walkabout? It seemed so to the fourteen thousand.

But then Miss Unpredictable rifled a passing backhand down the line for a fourth match point. It was an edge her legion of supporters desperately wanted her to capitalize upon before she started thinking about shopping later at Harrod's or looking in the windows in Knightsbridge.

So what happened at this crisis moment? Why, Margaret double-faulted. Game, set and match.

With winnings of $4320—Wimbledon's pay scale for women was slow to achieve status—Evonne bought her mother the first refrigerator she'd ever owned.

Victory was followed by endorsement offers too. Goolagong joined Mark McCormack's firm, International Management Incorporated, one athlete among a hundred or so to enlist with the Cleveland lawyer who started out in the early 1960s as Arnold Palmer's representative and prospered.

So did Goolagong. In the ensuing half dozen years her star climbed on the court and off, the money rolled in and some of her matches with a youngster from Florida, Christine Marie Evert, were absolute classics. By August 1977 she was a world figure, married, retired, a mother, and she was now back on the courts again whacking a crosscourt forehand that her opponent couldn't reach. Her opponent was bigger and stronger and tougher but he was no match for her.

"She's killing me," grinned Roger Cawley, her puffing husband, walking from the court in Toronto. "She's running me all over the court. But that's how she's getting back in form."

In this fashion, Cawley was highly instrumental in the return to form of Evonne Goolagong. Before they invaded Toronto for the Canadian championships they'd worked at their home on Hilton Head Island across a few miles of water from Savannah, Georgia.

And she came back, all right. The Cawleys went to Australia for the winter season there, then rejoined the Virginia Slims circuit that spring in America. Evonne won twenty-five straight matches in nailing down four tournaments, including an easy win over the Rabbit, Wendy Turnbull, the Forest Hills finalist in 1977, in the Slims final in Fort Lauderdale for a $20,000 pickup in Florida in January. She showed fine early form at Wimbledon in 1978 too, but a leg injury rendered her almost immobile in the latter stages of a semifinal match with the ultimate champion, Martina Navratilova. Was she thrilled that her game had come back so well?

"No, I'm thrilled about being a very good mother," bubbled the curly haired girl from the Australian outback. "I sort of feel like a whole person, you know? I didn't win at Wimbledon and I may not win the American championship—ever." She seemed struck by a sudden thought. "If I never win it," Evonne Goolagong laughed, "do you think it will matter to Kelly?"

*Billie Jean King*

# BILLIE JEAN KING

## [1943–        ]

No one ever really knows if the best athlete of one generation is better than the best of another for the obvious reason that they can't go out and settle the whole business in competition.

So whether Billie Jean King could step onto a tennis court and beat Suzanne Lenglen or Helen Wills or Maureen Connolly with each player at her absolute peak is something that can never be resolved.

But there's not much question that Billie Jean made as significant and lasting a contribution to women's tennis as any player in history and a considerably greater one than most. And along with that, since the proposition can't be proven, who's to say she wasn't the best player of them all?

Her record stands tall beside anyone's: six singles championships at Wimbledon, four at Forest Hills, the national champion of Australia, France and Italy; nineteen titles overall at Wimbledon (the six singles plus nine doubles and four mixed) and a remarkable sweep of all three titles at both Wimbledon and Forest Hills in 1967, and this is a list which disregards all the lesser tournaments on the women's professional curcuit where mere money was the reward. By 1971 she had become the first woman athlete to have earned $100,000 in a year.

Off the court the outspoken Billie Jean made herself the leading apostle of the movement to bring women's earnings closer to men's on the grounds that their box-office attractiveness was as powerful and therefore that they deserved equal purses. It was never her claim that women played the game better than men, or that they could beat men—only that they were as entertaining for the people who paid to get in.

Her campaign coincided with the women's liberation movement of the early 1970s. She was Gloria Steinem in sneakers. But she was not someone who felt no woman should ever again cast a shadow across a kitchen.

"If a woman wants to have a career I say fine, don't put her down for it," she said once. "If she wants to be a housewife, right on; if she wants to be a mother, beautiful. I want every woman to be able to be whatever she wants to be. That's what the women's movement is all about. All we want is for every woman to be able to pursue whatever career or personal lifestyle she chooses without fear of sexual discrimination."

As the most influential figure in the popularization of the women's game, she helped engineer the most talked-about coup in tennis when in September 1973 she played fifty-five-year-old Bobby Riggs in a crazy promotion from the Houston Astrodome that somehow caught the imagination of people across the continent, a Battle of the Sexes on the tennis court whose timing was perfect in establishing it as a sort of symbol of women's emancipation.

In the weeks leading up to the match there was more hype and ballyhoo than most heavyweight championship fights involving the extravagant Muhammad Ali usually generated, a lot of it inspired by nonstop Riggs talking and hamming his way from coast to coast but much of it given a subtly effective assist by the queen of tennis herself.

In an opulent South Carolina outpost called Hilton Head Island, Billie Jean prepared for the greatest male-female confrontation since Delilah took the shears to Samson. There, she was surrounded by the Atlantic Ocean, forests of live oak and palmetto trees, one husband, one secretary, one agent, one public-relations firm, three doctors and an occasional breakthrough of sanity.

At times, shielded by all of these forces at Hilton Head except sanity, Billie Jean was a mighty mysterious figure during the week before the Riggs match. On the one hand she kept appearing publicly in a bizarre tennis confection concocted by ABC Television, and on the other hand she kept rushing off to her chambers with an attack of at least the vapours, refusing to talk to anyone save, presumably, one or more of her doctors.

For two days she was reported to be suffering from stomach flu, then a mysterious virus, then something called hypoglycemia, which is a sugar deficiency in the blood, the opposite of diabetes. Periodically, though, she'd emerge from behind the medical reports and tear around the tennis court in this implausible ABC tournament and suddenly, after forty-eight hours of now-you-see-her-now-you-don't, she sat down calmly one evening and had a long friendly chat with a handful of newshounds.

There, removed from the high wall of humanity that was running her business life at that period, Billie Jean

King emerged as a straightforward person with no noticeable guile and small bombast. She talked matter-of-factly of the role she was playing in turning women's tennis into the first pro sport to challenge men's economic dominance.

"I'm a leader," she said. "Some of the women players have been critical of me but I notice they aren't turning down the attention or the checks they're getting."

She made the point that Riggs and tens of thousands of men had misconstrued the arguments she'd been advancing on behalf of women's tennis since the late 1960s. "Technically, women play sounder tennis because we're not as strong physically. Things they can do with a flick of the wrist we have to do with technique and execution. What men do with power we do with finesse and dexterity. With us, everything has to be a little surer.

"But the attraction of this match is that it's man against woman. Americans love fads, something new. I hear people are betting like crazy, dumb little his-her bets. That adds something extra. It's like horse races or like at Wimbledon where they wager a few bob on this one or that one. It adds excitement."

She ran her fingers through her dark brown short hair from time to time, combing it through from her forehead straight back. Almost everyone who ever wrote about Billie Jean King from the time she first hit tennis prominence took time out to observe that she was more appealing in the flesh than on television or in photographs. "Off the court," wrote Joe Hyams in *Playboy* in 1975, "she is soft, feminine, sexy—despite the glasses, a broad beam and a flat chest." Hyams, once a Hollywood columnist for the old New York *Herald-Tribune,* said that every time he saw Billie Jean she reminded him of Grace Kelly "who had equally unimpressive vital statistics but was all woman—no question about it."

On the tennis court she appeared shorter and stockier than close-up (she's five-feet-five in her tennis shoes and 137 pounds), mostly because her undercarriage was heavier than her superstructure, thighs and calves as tough-looking as a halfback's.

On the court too she was frequently given to walking around with her head down, her jaw working, berating herself. Her temper flared when she made a bad shot and she'd pounce on the ball impulsively and hammer it far over the stands. Nobody could understand these outbursts when she played Wimbledon; in her early years as a champion there the English crowds loved her outgoing personality, the sudden revelations of her inner struggle or elation, but temper tantrums were not the English way.

In conversation, once she had become the voice for women's emancipation, she was usually calm and articulate and bright, the blue eyes expressive behind the large round gold-rimmed glasses. By the time she was thirty in 1973 she was not quite the kid next door but when she called herself the Old Lady, which she had begun to do, she was serving a fault too. She was given to talking reflectively on what her efforts had contributed to women athletes.

"I've helped take the stigma off them," she said solemnly in that period. "There's no more of this 'You Amazons' bit, all the negative connotations are gone, or are certainly going. In that sense, I've made it better for young girls who want to be athletes, just as the women's movement itself helps people have a fuller life. With a little understanding people can love each other a lot more. That's pretty corny but it's how I feel."

Preparing for Riggs, the first intimation that Billie Jean might not be in top form came when she defaulted a match with Julie Heldman in the U.S. nationals at Forest Hills a couple of weeks before the Houston date, bowing out of the match in the third set. Then she showed up at Hilton Head along with seven other of the world's top players—Rod Laver, John Newcombe, Stan Smith, Arthur Ashe, Margaret Court, Evonne Goolagong and Chris Evert—for something called the World Invitation Tennis Classic.

This was a tournament with more wrinkles than Bobby Riggs's neck, a three-day roundelay of singles, doubles and mixed doubles available to the public at ten dollars a day and at the same time sold to ABC television for a series of one-hour telecasts to be released seven months later, one a week for eleven weeks.

So far, so good. But now here came the Hilton Head Company, a real-estate development firm hoping to capitalize on the TV exposure the following summer, endeavoring to compel news people to sign a document declaring that no scores would be published until the conclusion of the telecasts almost a year later. Here was the silly spectacle of the world's top players shooting for $150,000 in prize money in front of fifteen hundred paying spectators, and reporters being told to keep results a secret as a favor to television.

In this weird setting, then, Billie Jean took the court in the opening match opposed by young Evert and won the first set 6–4 and was leading 5–3 in the second when she suddenly came undone, double-faulting twice at match point, losing the set and then being run off the court in the third by 6–1.

Whereupon she was whisked by her blond twenty-eight-year-old lawyer husband, Larry King, to a townhouse set deep amid pines, palmettos, doctors and assorted fauna, and reports on her condition began emerging. A mixed-doubles match was washed out but, out of deference to television, not defaulted, simply postponed. This was some tennis tournament, all right. "No interviews," announced Billie Jean King's husband, an emancipated man wearing a frown.

Next day, while the world waited, who should turn up in a television booth hung high in the trees at one end of the court but herself, the ailing queen, all tanned and freckled.

"She's not talking to anybody," Billie Jean King's husband told reporters. "No interviews."

At which moment the ailing queen stepped nimbly down from the trees, took up her tennis racquet, charged all over the court in partnering Arthur Ashe in a three-set victory over Smith and Evert, and then strolled calmly into the clubhouse, wiping perspiration from her forehead. She extended a firm hand to greet interviewers and said she was sorry she had kept them waiting.

"What would you like to ask me?" smiled Billie Jean King warmly.

Billie Jean Moffitt was her name until she met Larry King at Los Angeles State College and married him on September 17, 1965, two months before she turned twenty-two. He was a prelaw student one year her junior. The newlyweds moved into a tiny apartment near the campus where Billie Jean kept house through the first fall and winter of their marriage. That's how her mother had done it, and that's how Billie Jean felt it ought to be done: a woman's place was in the home.

Billie Jean's mother stayed home until her two children were out from under her apron and then she took a job as a receptionist at a medical center. Billie Jean's father was an engineer with the fire department. The family home was Long Beach, California, where Billie Jean and her brother Randy were born, and it turned out that both were excellently coordinated athletes. One day Randy pitched three no-hitters and a one-hitter in a baseball tournament in Long Beach, and some years later while his sister was burgeoning as a tennis star Randy was finding his way to the majors relief pitching for the San Francisco Giants. Billie Jean might have made the majors too: she was one hell of a shortstop, and her father recalled after she became a Wimbledon champion that at fire department picnics the men always wanted her plugging up the left side of the infield.

But baseball's loss was tennis's gain when Billie Jean decided she wanted to be in a sport "where you could be a lady," as she phrased it in her pre-emancipation period. It was her parents who suggested tennis, and when she was eleven her father, Willard J. Moffitt, enrolled her in the city's community program.

"There was no stopping her," Willard remembered once. "Neither my wife nor I ever played tennis and this made her love for the sport quite surprising to us. She played tennis every day during the summer and after school and weekends while attending high school. She said there wasn't anything more in the world she wanted than to play some day at Wimbledon."

But before she turned all her zeal and energy to tennis she had loved football as much as baseball and running against boys in track meets as much as both.

"The first time I saw a professional baseball game with my father, what struck me like a thunderbolt was that there were no women on that baseball diamond," Billie Jean recalled years later. "My ambition to become a ballplayer was shattered. Throughout my adolescence I found a subtle social pressure against being an athlete. I decided on tennis because it was, and still is, more acceptable as a sport for girls."

She won her first championship in 1958, the under-fifteen title of Southern California, then lost in the national quarterfinals. "I was very erratic when I started playing tournaments," she said a decade later, "and I suffered. I couldn't stand to lose. It used to *kill* me! But I felt in the long run that if I really wanted to achieve my goals I would have to lose."

A year later, in 1959, she met the Wimbledon champion Maria Bueno in the Eastern Grass Courts championship at South Orange, and though she was handled easily by the dancing Brazilian her play impressed a prominent eastern seaboard coach Frank Brennan who took on development of her game. A year later his guidance helped her reach the national under-eighteen final where she was nipped by Karen Hantze. A year after that she and Hantze became the youngest pair ever to win the women's doubles title at Wimbledon. Billie Jean was seventeen.

And then in 1962 she scored sensationally at Wimbledon, beating Margaret Smith, who became Margaret Court, the defending champion's first match on the hallowed grass that year. King was eighteen, knocking off the incumbent in the first round for the first time ever at Wimbledon. And though she accounted for the champion in the upset of the tournament, she was not impressed with her progress.

"From 1961 to 1964 my tennis never got any worse, but it never got any better, either," she wrote in her memoirs with Kim Chapin in 1974, a volume called, not to make matters obscure, *Billie Jean*. "I was winning my share of singles titles on the grass-court circuit and other places but by the end of 1964, even though I'd been playing internationally for four years, I still hadn't won a major singles title. In 1962 I'd beaten Margaret Smith at Wimbledon but I didn't beat her again for four years and lost fourteen consecutive matches to her in the interim."

Two things turned her around: she undertook three months of intensive training in Australia with the one-time Aussie Davis Cupper Mervyn Rose, and she lost to Margaret Court at Forest Hills in 1964. Each was important in the greening of Billie Jean King.

The turnaround began in 1964 when she quit school ("I realized that for me college was a farce; for starters, I wasn't learning anything") and accepted the backing of an Australian businessman and tennis buff, Robert Mitchell, to work there with Rose. Mitchell lived in the wealthy Melbourne suburb of Toorak and had a court on his property. King and Rose had a private tennis session every morning, and in the afternoon an Aussie player,

Owen Davidson or Roy Emerson or whoever, usually dropped by to rally.

Rose worked on King's forehand and her serve—and her weight. He made her run to get in shape and slim down, shortened the backswing on her serve while directing her to toss the ball higher, and actually revolutionized the forehand.

"On the backswing he had me do this funny thing, like sort of bring the racquet back as though I were pulling a sword from a block of stone and then swing forward right from the hip," King once recalled. She was hitting her forehands with her wrist laid back too, instead of having the racquet out ahead of it. He also taught her tactics on an advanced scale. It was a drastic three months and Rose said it would take another six months of patient practice for the changes to become effective.

Being in Australia in winter, she toured on the Aussie summer circuit (the seasons are screwy down there) and she lost to everybody in sight, including a fourteen-year-old. And she once served thirty-five double faults in a match.

But by fall, as promised, things were beginning to happen. Indeed, they were beginning to happen that summer at Wimbledon. That's when she encountered Margaret Court, and although she was beaten she never looked back. How come?

"In the first eight games I played fantastically well and built a 5-3 lead but lost the set 8-6," she recalled. "The same thing happened in the second set: I had a 5-3 lead and even got to 40-15, double set point, and lost 7-5. Margaret picked herself up and I didn't. I played carefully and didn't cut loose. Certain players never develop this ability. They play brilliantly and steadily to the last point and then they choke, which is what I had been doing.

"During the trophy presentation I realized I'd had the match in my hands and didn't go for the kill. I knew then I could beat Margaret—and anyone else in the world."

She could too, the way it turned out, but in 1966 there was still the matter of proving it: she still hadn't won a major championship. She got her chance in early July when she won through to the final at Wimbledon. There she was opposed by the graceful Maria Bueno—a meeting, as one of the French correspondents noted, of the gym teacher and the *professeur de violin.*

They played on a warm and windy afternoon, both cautious, though no one understood why the Brazilian ballerina played tentatively since she was by now a three-time singles champion at Wimbledon. Perhaps it was because King had the palpable support of a gallery filled with people who had enjoyed her ebullience through the 1960s and still regarded her as a bouncing determined upset-maker, exhorting herself, spanking her thigh, grimacing, grinning, her personality visible as a cross-court backhand.

She was the first to settle into stride, volleying winners that kept Bueno on the defensive, and lobbing deep when Maria went to the net. King raced off with the first set but Bueno got her overhead in working order to turn King's lobs into swishing winners and square the match.

After that, playing grimly, King gave Bueno no opportunity to get off the defensive. The senorita won only one game in the deciding set. So finally, at twenty-two, Billie Jean had her first major singles title.

The following year marked the beginning of serious problems with her knees though she continued to play and to win when she wasn't approaching surgery or recovering from it. She had one operation in 1968 and another in 1970. She came back strongly each time, delighting in the game, enchanted by the rare moment when she'd hit the perfect shot.

In later years she occasionally rejoiced in retelling the most satisfying shot she ever hit. It was in the 1972 Wimbledon final against Evonne Goolagong, a match she was scrambling to win.

"I kept going down the line with my backhand—that's the percentage shot—but there was just enough of a crosswind to hold the ball up in the air long enough for Evonne to run it down," she remembered, playing out this shot.

"So I waited and told myself that on match point I'd do just the opposite and bomb a crosscourt shot. I served. She returned to my backhand and I snapped a short top-spin shot cross court, catching her off balance, preparing to cover the line. My shot was a winner. I threw my racquet in the air and thought, 'I did it! I hit a perfect shot!' "

By 1967, collecting more and more attention, King was muttering darkly and publicly about the hypocrisy of amateur tennis, the under-the-table payoffs, and the standing joke that most players didn't want to turn pro because they'd have to take a cut in pay. Top players could make $1000 a week by agreeing to enter this tournament and that one. King argued that open tennis would remove the sham from shamateur. Whenever she won a big tournament she got on this theme to the press.

She said once she didn't think U.S. Davis Cup players should receive per diem expense money on a year-round basis and still be called amateurs. She risked a suspension from the USLTA for sounding off but none came, partly because open tennis arrived first. The British Lawn Tennis Association voted for it in December 1967, meaning the 1968 Wimbledon would be open, and when the International Lawn Tennis Federation agreed in March 1968 to go along, the sham was over.

Did that delight and silence Billie Jean? Of course. For nearly a month. In April the first open tournament in tennis history was held, the British hard-court championships at Bournemouth, England. When King observed that Ken Rosewall won $2400 as men's singles winner and Virginia Wade $720 as women's, she had a new platform.

Worse was to come. King won her first Italian championship in 1970 and got $600. Ilie Nastase collected $3500 for beating Jan Kodes in the men's final. And a few months later during the national championships at Forest Hills, the prize-money list was posted for the Pacific Southwest tournament promoted by Jack Kramer in Los Angeles—a $12,500 prize for the men's *winner* and a grand *total* of $7500 for the women to scamper for.

King was convinced Kramer was inflexible in his opposition to women's equality on the courts (later, in her Astrodome match with Riggs, she refused to go on the court until ABC removed Kramer from the telecast crew) so she and three other leaders of the women's battle, Rosie Casals, Francoise Durr and Ann Jones, recruited

Gladys Heldman as an ally. Heldman, founder and editor of *Tennis World* magazine, readily went to California to appeal to Kramer for an adjustment in the purse structure but the former top internationalist and tour promoter declined. So Heldman talked with Joseph Cullman, chairman of the board of the Philip Morris tobacco company, who agreed to sponser a tournament exclusively for women on dates overlapping the Kramer event, and named it for the company's Virginia Slims cigarettes.

That marked the birth of the Slims tour that became the backbone of women's pro tennis. Billie Jean, the top women's player, toured, talked, promoted and played every waking hour, criss-crossing the country. Every town they hit, King, Casals, Jones and/or Durr spurned sleep to visit newspaper offices and radio and television stations, spreading the word in unending interviews. Billie Jean, as the Wimbledon and Forest Hills star and the first woman to pass $100,000 in pro sports earnings, was always top copy, and her controversial outspokenness on all topics didn't hurt either. She was hot on the court too. She won nineteen of thirty Slims tournaments the first year and twelve of twenty-seven in 1972.

Her success cost her, though. Jealousies cropped up among women players who weren't getting the attention or money that accrued to Number One. King related in her memoirs that her position cost her the friendship of Kristien Kemmer, "the one person I could trust." She'd known Kemmer for a number of years and they'd often gone to each other for advice. "But one day she popped up and said it was over," King wrote. "She said her goal was to be Number One and we just couldn't spend a lot of time together any more."

Her aggressiveness cost the Old Lady on the court too. Crowds, especially Wimbledon crowds, loved her when she was a determined, scowling, thigh-slapping underdog—a sort of yappy puppy—but once she switched from underdog to top dog those antics weren't nearly so endearing. "You've got to learn—and it's a hard lesson—that when you get to the top of the ladder, a great many people line up to see you fall."

But the game never ceased to fascinate her even as she moved toward her mid-thirties. After she won her sixth Wimbledon singles title in 1975 she announced that that was it, she wasn't playing in the big ones any more. Her wonky knees were troubling her and a year later she added more zipper scars to her kneecap by having her third operation. But after a layoff, she took her announcement back. She started working herself into playing condition again. By then she was up to her eyeballs in King Enterprises with husband Larry, a multimillion dollar business built around her tennis racquet and including endorsements of products ranging from tennis equipment to suntan lotion, the publishing of a magazine *WomenSports* and an involvement in World Team Tennis, a circuit launched by the Kings in 1974.

In 1978, almost back in top playing condition, she confessed that nothing she'd encountered was tougher than coming back after knee surgery. "You work and work and it's so *slow,* and I'm not the most patient person in the world," she wailed. "But I'm stubborn enough to continue the pain and the drudgery and the therapy. The only way you can get through it is by thinking of the end result."

So why?

"Because there's nothing else quite like it, being an athlete and having that experience of being in motion, being able to run and feel the wind in your hair and all those sensations. It's music, it's dancing, it's the greatest thing in the whole wide world."

*Chris Evert*

# CHRIS EVERT

## [1954–    ]

CHRISTINE MARIE EVERT didn't simply arrive on the national tennis scene in the United States; no, she exploded onto it. One minute she was a pig-tailed, poker-faced, sixteen-year-old schoolgirl not widely known beyond the clay courts of her native Florida and the next moment she was on the stadium court of Forest Hills, the salvation of the 1971 U.S. Open Championships.

There, she was relentlessly pursued by camera crews and magazine writers and autograph seekers. She had been thrust into this spotlight by a tournament director, Billy Talbert, who recognized a hot property when he saw one. He sent her to center stage in every one of her matches, even in the first round of the first tournament of her first visit to what was then America's foremost tennis setting. Chris Evert saved the tournament and, in turn, the tournament launched Chris Evert.

Precipitating this unusual turn was the fact that open tennis, inaugurated in Britain in 1968, was still damp behind the ears three years later, feeling its way and filled with factions. Pros who had joined World Championship Tennis boycotted Forest Hills to protest a decision by the International Lawn Tennis Federation to ban WCT players from open tournaments because some had bypassed tournaments backed by the United States Lawn Tennis Association.

Thus the Grand Slam star Rod Laver and his countryman Ken Rosewall, the defending champion, were absent. Other stars were too. There was a shortage of top women players, for other reasons. Defending champion Margaret Court was pregnant, Evonne Goolagong had returned to Australia after a smashing triumph at Wimbledon, and Virginia Wade, the best Briton, was injured.

"The championships, threatened by tedium, bogged down by controversy, and eventually awash in rain, will be remembered as the one spurned by the big names and brought to life by a little girl," Roy Blount wrote.

The little girl, Evert, was riding a string of forty-four straight winning matches, all on clay and almost all on Florida clay. What brought her a faint ray of hope on Forest Hills grass was that she'd walloped Wade in straight sets in a Wightman Cup match a month earlier at Cleveland.

People were curious about the schoolgirl, and responded quickly to the setting tournament director Talbert supplied for her. The youngster, who said later of her stadium court prominence, "I was petrified," did not disappoint. She beat German Edda Buding easily, then survived six match points against a highly-rated grass player, Mary Ann Curtis, and won in three sets by 4–6, 7–6, 6–1.

The match solidified Evert's place in the headlines. All those saved match points by a cool impassive kid patiently hammering two-handed backhands and looping forehands deep against the baseline were all the fans—and the headline writers and camera crews—needed.

For icing on the cake she came from behind twice more. She beat two internationally known players, France's Francoise Durr and Australia's Lesley Hunt, after losing the first set in each match. She wasn't a spectacular player, but who cared? Her tactics rarely varied. She hugged the baseline and slammed her ground strokes deep to the corners across the net, running her opponents until they drooped and faded and toppled. That was fodder enough for the TV audience. In that one tournament Chrissiemania was born. Its swirl helped sweep her into the semifinals of her country's most important tournament against Billie Jean King.

By then, though, players were beginning to grumble, claiming Evert's prominence was unjustified, that her two-handed backhand was garbage, that she was so intent on her own game she often served before her opponents reached position. Billie Jean took the long view. "Chris has really helped women's tennis," she said, "What it needs is more personalities. If the other girls feel jealous about the attention she's received, they should stop and think beyond their own little worlds."

Billie Jean wasn't quite so charitable on the court, naturally. She kept Chris's rhythm disrupted with a variety of speeds and spins and dropshots. With her tough serves and with lobs off Evert's returns of the dropshots she was able to keep command in straight sets, 6–3, 6–2. What her lobs revealed was that the kid from Florida had a lousy overhead.

By then the boom was launched. Chrissie, as everyone was calling her, went back to Fort Lauderdale's St. Thomas Aquinas high school, turned seventeen on December 21 and learned she'd been ranked No. 16 in the

U.S. A year later she went to Wimbledon for the first time and reached the semifinals before falling to Evonne Goolagong in a thrilling match between the two youngest rising stars. That year Evert climbed to No. 3 in the national rankings at home while declining, as an amateur, money she'd otherwise earn in tournaments. By her eighteenth birthday that December she'd passed up more than $50,000. But as soon as she turned professional the money began to roll in.

By 1975 she was ranked first in the world, a pinnacle she achieved again in 1976 and again in 1977. In 1978 most people rated her No. 1 after she disposed of Martina Navratilova in the first U.S. Open ever held in the new Flusing Meadows setting, the successor to famed old Forest Hills. But Evert, who had lost to the Czech lefthander Navratilova at Wimbledon three months earlier, said she thought she ought to share the top spot with Martina.

Chris won Wimbledon in 1974 and 1976 and Forest Hills in the famous stadium's final three tournaments for the national championships, 1975 through 1977. By April 1978 she had a winning streak on clay of an improbable one hundred and eighteen consecutive matches, and had won twenty-four straight tournaments. And what *that* added up to were two hundred and thirty-six winning sets and a mere five lost ones.

In winning this twenty-fourth tournament Evert disposed of Kerry Melville Reid in the final of a $125,000 event at Hilton Head Island. "On clay it's just about impossible to beat Chris," Reid reflected wanly. "You have to have patience and be willing to stand out there all day. I don't think the tour players are physically tough enough to do it or mentally tough enough to do it. Everything I tried she had an answer for. She's just so solid."

Evert grew up pounding a tennis ball on clay in Florida where her father Jimmy became teaching professional in the mid 1940s at a public courts club called Holiday Park in Fort Lauderdale. She always conceded that clay, with its slow bounces that enabled her to reach almost anything, was the best playing surface for her game, though obviously, with her record, it was the rare player who beat her on any surface.

"I really enjoy playing on clay, I can be more creative, I can do whatever I want with the tennis ball, I can handle any situation," she told Julie Heldman in *World Tennis* in 1978, soon after she'd been acclaimed as top player in the world for the third straight year. "Do I sound conceited? Actually, it's a very nice confidence that I only get to feel at clay tournaments. If I play Goolagong or Navratilova or King on grass or indoor Sporteze I still surprise myself when I win. I know they'd beat me if I didn't use my head and my heart."

For all her surpassing skill Evert was a hard player for the galleries to take to after the cute little button stage of her mid-teens. Once crowds became familiar with her implacable pursuit of victory, her cool executioner's stoicism, they felt remote, made more so, perhaps, by her impeccable appearance—full makeup, earrings, a necklace, a bracelet, a ribbon in her honey-colored braid or bun. "At the end of a match an opponent often looked as though she had combed her hair with an eggbeater," Grace Lichtenstein wrote in the book on women's tennis. "Chris looked as if she had just left Elizabeth Arden's."

Evert played the game without exhilaration or even any

sign of enjoyment. She played with impassive efficiency, a manner taught by her father. Early on, she learned the value of concentration and discipline on a tennis court.

"From the moment she walks on the court for a match she is all business," Herbert Warren Wind said of her in the *New Yorker*. "She has no convenient smiles for the spectators. She is completely wrapped up in the task at hand. Though she is not as poker-faced as Helen Wills was, she shows little emotion on court. Every now and then after losing a point she feels she should have won, Chris will frown a little and twist her shoulders around quickly as she walks to the baseline, but that is about the extent of her histrionics. She is an unfailingly courteous and gracious competitor but because she devotes her attention exclusively to playing tennis and remains so cool and unsweaty, galleries have a tendency to overlook these attributes."

Evert was aware she projected a frosty image, and was prepared to settle for it. "Sometimes I wish I could be more outgoing and express myself on the court," she said once, "but most of the time I'm glad I keep it inside. I don't want too many people taking a piece of me, knowing me too well."

As a private person she was at ease with her family and close friends, but the public never got a glimpse of that side of her. They flocked to her matches but they usually cheered against the mechanical woman at the baseline. Inside, she was aware of the crowd's mood and sometimes it dismayed her. "If I'm playing a foreign player and the crowd isn't for me I feel like screaming at the people, 'Hey, I'm an American! Why don't you cheer for me?' Ninety-five percent of the time when the crowd's against me it makes me tougher. I don't want to give them the satisfaction of seeing me lose."

Tennis fans could hardly guess the depth of Evert's emotion because Evert so seldom let them see any. In this she took after her father, a man of calm reserve, stockily built with the same brisk pigeon-toed walk millions of people became familiar with watching his daughter in televised tennis matches. Jimmy Evert got interested in tennis as a youngster living in Chicago across the street from a tennis club where he got a job as a ball boy. He went to Notre Dame on a tennis scholarship, reached No. 11 in the U.S. in his peak years in the early 1950s.

By then he and his wife Colette had moved to Florida where he was the manager and teaching pro at the public courts club. Chris was to become noted for her two-handed backhand but this wasn't her father's doing.

"Chrissie started playing when she was six and really couldn't hit a backhand with one hand," he recalled once. "She just wasn't strong enough. So the two-hander was a good instrument for her, and is for all little kids that age, though now everybody, large and small, is using it because of Chrissie's success, and Borg's and Jimmy Connors's."

The senior Evert wasn't at all familiar with the two-hander. "The Australian, John Bromwich, was the only player I know of who hit his backhand with two hands in my time," he remembered. "Chrissie, as I say, just couldn't lift the racquet any other way. And when she got good at it, why would I change her?"

However, in 1972 after Chris's explosive introduction at Forest Hills, Billie Jean King was highly critical of the two-hander.

"It shouldn't be taught to kids," she growled. "The trouble with it is that it establishes a weakness."

Jimmy Evert accepted that criticism. But he calmly added: "Necessity is the mother of invention. Chrissie wouldn't be the player she is unless she used the two-hander. She's not a great athlete, not in the sense Billie Jean and Virginia Wade are great athletes. But she has remarkable concentration and great anticipation."

She learned these qualities, or at least honed them if they are innate, at her father's knee at Holiday Park, though in no sense was her father a tennis version of a stage mother, pushing the prodigy toward prominence at every opportunity. Tennis was secondary to education, for example.

"My parents told me if I didn't make the honor roll at school I wouldn't be allowed out," she recalled once. And she enjoyed hanging out at Holiday Park, an airy, grassy expanse with a couple of dozen clay courts lined neatly in one area of the park, with a clubhouse and a practice wall and the courts alive with players. In the late 1970s Jimmy Evert was there still, white-haired, darkly tanned in white shorts, white T-shirt, white tennis shoes, arms folded across his chest embracing a Chris Evert–model Wilson tennis racquet as he stood at the baseline of a practice court carefully watching the technique of the young people he gave lessons to.

The five Evert kids were familiar with Holiday Park, Chris the oldest girl, a year younger than brother Drew, three years ahead of sister Jeanne, six ahead of brother John and thirteen ahead of sister Clare, who was born in 1968. The two boys had state tennis rankings in their age groups, and in 1972 Jeanne was runner-up in the sixteen-and-under girls' national championship. Jeanne turned pro and toured with Chris in the mid-1970s (she was ranked No. 15 in the U.S. in 1976) but a lack of height hurt her advancement.

Chris began playing in 1960, discovered one day by her father hitting balls against the big concrete wall at the courts. Jimmy showed her the proper way to do things. Liking what she was doing, little Chris practiced longer and longer and harder and harder. Half a dozen years later she was hammering tennis balls two to three hours a day after school and eight hours over weekends.

If the public wasn't conscious of her name when she showed up at Forest Hills in 1971, tennis buffs were. She had won several age-group titles, and in the fall of 1970, not yet sixteen, she scored an upset over Margaret Court in a tournament in Charlotte, North Carolina. Court had just won a marvellous Wimbeldon final from Billie Jean King, an emotional energy-draining struggle, by marathon scores of 14–12, 11–9. Thus, she wasn't in much of a frame of mind to get steamed up over a match with a fifteen-year-old unknown.

But in April 1971 Chris won a Virginia Slims tournament in Florida and in August she was chosen, on the strength of this, to compete against Great Britain in the Wightman Cup matches. Carole Graebner, the team captain who made the selection, confessed she'd never seen the youngster play "but everybody's talking about her." With the United States leading by three matches to two in this best-of-seven event Evert played Virginia Wade. When she dismantled the black-haired Briton with loss of a mere two games, her win gave the Americans their thirty-sixth triumph in forty-three attempts with the Brits.

Then she went into the stadium court at Forest Hills and in short order captured everyone's attention as no other young American had done in years. "The Ice Maiden," Bud Collins called her in the Boston *Globe*. Larry Merchant wrote in the New York *Post:* "She plays with a brass metronome ticking inside her. Playing her is like playing a wall; the ball comes back, inevitably, incessantly."

After Billie Jean beat her there they met on Fort Lauderdale clay the following February. Evert won easily. "I don't know how anybody can beat her on clay," King said, the first in a long line of players to utter that sentence. King winced a few years later over the memory of that match, a 6–1, 6–0 lacing. "That's the worst beating I ever got, even as a junior."

Through the spring of 1972 anticipation grew for a meeting between Evert and another sensational youngster, Goolagong, who'd upset defending champion Margaret Court at Wimbledon the previous July. The young women looked forward to meeting too; they'd become aware of each other.

At last they met at the Maureen Connolly Brinker International in March 1972. But the meeting turned out to be social. Billie Jean took care of that: she beat both en route to a tournament victory. So their first encounter from opposite sides of a tennis net was reserved for Wimbledon in July that year when they were semifinalists and, understandably, the center of intense media attention, a twenty- and a seventeen-year-old, unquestionably the best players of the future.

It was quite a match.

"For ninety-five minutes we ran, stretched, lunged and sprawled," Goolagong recalled once. "We bent, hammered, smashed, stroked, nursed and blasted balls over the net, producing the kind of drawn-out spectacular points that make tennis excruciating for spectators."

In Evert, Goolagong soon found what people had been marvelling at, a youngster who stood at the baseline and pelted sizzling passing shots or dinked deceptive dropshots barely across the cord. She showed great balance and timing, and an anticipation that enabled her to reach the ball and set herself before exploding a return. She won the first set by 6–4 and then she boomed into a 3–0 lead in the second.

But Goolagong was not quite ready to be swept away. She began laying a crosscourt backhand short to Evert's two-handed side, as her coach and guardian Vic Edwards had advised in analyzing how Evert's baseline broadsides might be dampened. It was the most awkward stroke for a two-hander to come to grips with, forcing that player to stretch wide and reach low for returns. So Goolagong came on, rebounding so brilliantly that she won six straight games and leveled the match.

The third set was hectic, each breaking the other's serve with occasional determined bursts, and they climbed to 4–4, neither able to make the commanding move. Serving the ninth game, Goolagong rushed behind her first serve and was able to catch Evert short and put away enough winning volleys to get ahead 5–4. Now she recognized the critical moment for the break that would decide the match.

"All afternoon she'd been killing me with that cute deceptive drop shot, halting a big swing abruptly to deliver a wristy flick," Goolagong noted later. "She tried it a last time. I sprinted ahead as she caressed the ball. It was barely over the net. But I was there and turned it into an even weaker drop onto her side."

On the next point Evonne tried an unusual shot, a forehand crosscourt chop that died almost the moment it touched down. It was a winner, and now it was love-thirty. Then another of those short backhanders to Evert's two-hand side for love-forty, and then another and a volley to the open court for the match.

After a semifinal so fiery, the anticlimactic wrapup had Billie Jean catching Goolagong on the emotional slide and dumping her handily by 6–3 and 6–3, removing her Wimbledon title.

In ensuing years Evert and Goolagong engaged in classic matches, two marvellous ones two months apart in early summer 1976. In Los Angeles in April they toiled for three minutes less than two hours in the final of the $150,000 Virginia Slims championship and Goolagong wrested the $40,000 top prize by 6–3, 5–7, 6–4.

In the Wimbledon final in July, there they were at Centre Court, the two best women players the most revered tournament could produce. It stirred the capacity crowd all through the long afternoon and it wasn't decided until the impassive young woman from Florida broke Goolagong in the thirteenth game of the third set, then grimly made sure of her own service to bring off an

8–6 margin that finally allowed the fourteen thousand tense and rapt fans to let down.

Then twenty-one, Chris had taken on a certain sophistication in the wake of years of ingenuous travel. For a long time the culture of foreign lands was given no thought at all by her, as it was given no thought by most young tennis players far more intent on the tournaments than the countries staging them. Despite her maturity at tennis as a teen-ager, Evert was still a young girl, pleasant and unaffected off the court, the top of her dresser usually littered with eye shadow, mascara, lipstick and nail polish. Sight-seeing was confined to airports, hotel rooms and tennis clubs.

"Where's the McDonald's hamburger place?" she once asked the American player Brian Gottfried upon arrival in Paris.

"On the Champs Elysees," replied Gottfried, also from Fort Lauderdale. "You can't miss it."

As she matured she was somewhat of a loner on the tour. For awhile she hung out with Martina Navratilova, showing the young Czech around America. But that stopped when Martina beat her one night in straight sets in the final at Houston. She found she couldn't be too chummy with an opponent, the dichotomy of emotions was no good.

Indeed, Chris didn't want her emotions bothering her with any opponent. In the Virginia Slims Championship tournament in Los Angeles in 1976 she had a tough three-setter with blonde, frail-looking Sue Barker of England, pulling out the last set at 6–4.

"I felt kind of numb and that was a bad sign," Evert

reconstructed. "I had to start psyching myself up. I tried to get very mad. I have a tendency to sometimes dislike my opponents. That's part of the killer instinct. I want to beat them. With Sue it's tough to do that. She's not the type you want to hate out there."

After Navratilova, Evert's buddy became Kristien Kemmer, who had been close with Billie Jean until she advised King she was breaking off the friendship because she, Kemmer, wanted to replace her as No. 1. But Kemmer's game never carried her close to the exalted position. Later she married and, not being as threatening as Navratilova, was Evert's pal on the road. Then they too had a falling out and Rosie Casals became Evert's close friend.

"Rosie's so loyal, she'd give the shirt off her back to a friend," Chris reflected once. "That's why she's not No. 1. There's a selfish streak in all champions. I'll be the greatest friend, wife, mother when I'm retired, but it's so tough to be unselfish and giving when you're out there competing."

Evert and Jimmy Connors were engaged in 1975. "For a few years my whole life was tennis and Jimmy, and then there was a void there—no Jimmy," she told Julie Heldman. "After that, I started thinking about myself, my morals, my life, my future. Until then, my dad had made all the decisions, and I had agreed with everything. Now we have occasional outbursts, but we're closer as a result of them."

Though she and Connors cancelled marriage plans they remained friendly. Chris sat solemnly beside his mother Gloria during the Wimbledon singles final in

1978 when Bjorn Borg tore him to shreds in three one-sided sets and walked away with a third straight title there.

"One thing I've learned is that it's tough to have success without someone to share it with," the twenty-three-year-old millionaire Christine Marie Evert reflected. "I'd like to have someone to share it with but still retain my independence. I'm beginning to wonder if that's possible."

In 1979 it began to look like it. She became engaged to the Britisher John Lloyd, convinced this time that she had found what she'd been looking for.

*Martina Navratilova*

# MARTINA NAVRATILOVA

[1956–    ]

ONLY LIFE ITSELF is extraordinary enough to tolerate the story of Martina Navratilova; put it on the silver screen and audiences would either figure the plot an insult or laugh themselves into the aisles.

Here is a young woman behind the Iron Curtain, who has hidden, terrified, from Russian tanks, who has been hassled by the secret police of her native Czechoslovakia, who has defected to the free world and added thirty pounds surrounding hamburgers and pancakes as fast as she can swallow, and who has, within three years and by twenty-one, turned herself into the top woman in tennis and next thing to a millionaire. And knocked off the weight so that she's svelte as a cougar.

During six months of 1978 Navratilova revealed the fruits of a most impressive self-discipline. She won seven straight tournaments on the Virginia Slims professional circuit, then went to England and twice took charge of the reigning queen of world tennis, Chris Evert, the second time at Wimbledon, that most prestigious and nerve-testing tournament of all.

In winning there, Navratilova didn't go to pieces when adversity caught up to her as she'd done many, many times in previous years. In fact, quite the opposite; after falling behind by 2–4 in the deciding set and with the tension crackling, it was Navratilova who remained steady and took over, not Evert. Indeed, she played the way Evert was expected to, and in the closing climactic three games Martina won seven straight points, dropped one, and then won five in a row for the set and match.

The change in one year was remarkable. In 1977 at Wimbledon Navratilova faced Betty Stove in the quarterfinals and staggered and scrambled about the court, playing erratically against a tall powerful opponent renowned for her own unpredictability. Martina was leading 5–2 in the first set and lost it 9–8, won the second handily at 6–3, and then caved in, winning only one game in the third, behaving childishly, imploring the heavens to intervene, clasping her hand to her forehead and, when the match ended, dissolving in tears.

This was almost a repeat of her first-round behavior at Forest Hills in 1975 when she lost to Janet Newberry and, covering her head with a towel as she slumped into a chair at courtside, wept uncontrollably.

But, of course, she was not yet eighteen in September that year when she announced there at Forest Hills that she was not returning to Czechoslovakia. In the lonely year that followed she often questioned her wisdom in defecting. Cut off from home and family, she was rootless and confused. Small wonder she cried when her plans seemed to go awry. She soon was earning a good deal of money, but she was spending it almost as fast. Strong men winced when Martina Navratilova began to work her way through the junk food emporiums of North America—hamburgers, hot dogs, potato chips, pancakes, french fries, anything that didn't jump off her plate before she could devour it. Within months, eating like a linebacker, she weighed 172 pounds.

And on the court she was the terrible-tempered Miss Bang, headstrong, testy and impatient. Her impetuous style made her exciting to watch, but heaven help the linesperson who called a close one against her. Also, sure as hamburgers ought to contain onions, when Martina blew a match there was the inevitable flow of tears. She cried more than John's other wife in *John's Other Wife*.

"I was lonely," Martina related once to the columnist Red Smith. "I couldn't turn to my parents for help but I did have some good friends who helped. I defected because the Czech tennis federation wouldn't let me travel, especially to the United States. I was determined to be No. 1 and if I couldn't come here where ninety-five percent of the big tournaments are played, I had no chance. Yes, I had talked about it a little with my parents but I don't think they really believed I would do it. It was my decision and it was all a question of tennis. There was nothing political about it."

Political or not, Prague took her defection in tall umbrage. The controlled press of the industrially efficient and scenically beautiful country dominated by the Russians managed to publish papers day after day without bothering to mention her name, and foreign newspapers are scarcer than bikinied Eskimos in Czechoslovakia. Martina hoped her family had watched her match with Evert on German television, close to the frontier, but wasn't sure. "I'm very sad that I can't share this with them," she said after collecting her Wimbledon trophy from the Duchess of Kent. "I wanted them up there in the stand. It's practically impossible for me to go back.

The only way I can see them again is if they can leave." In a chat during the presentation ceremony the duchess said she would help if she could.

It was easy for a visitor to be confused in Prague that spring. It is the capital of a country that has produced many fine tennis players (Jaraslov Drobny shaded Ken Rosewall by 13–11, 4–6, 6–2, 9–7 in the 1954 Wimbledon final, and Jan Kodes handled Alexandre Metreveli 6–1, 9–8, 6–3 in 1973). Still, only an occasional tennis ball could be found in Prague department stores or in windows in uprooted Wenceslas Square where a new subway is endlessly under construction, the ball suspended from the ceiling on a long skinny elastic band. You couldn't buy a can of balls anywhere. In the stores the only tennis ball was the one you saw hanging there.

"Perhaps they will be in tomorrow," a clerk told visitors, day after day. Maybe they were, occasionally, but not often. It was next to impossible to buy tennis balls in Prague. So it seemed unlikely when Martina Navratilova became the first Czechoslovak woman to win a Wimbledon singles title (she had already won one in doubles) that little girls all over the country would turn to tennis. They might want to, if they knew she had won. There are beautiful courts of red clay to be seen in Prague, especially in the parks that decorate the city, but there were more tennis courts than tennis balls. The Russian overlords didn't put much of a priority on them, and stores weren't carrying imports from Dunlop or Slazenger or Wilson or the other western manufacturers. It had been this way through the decade following 1968 when the Russians put down the Czech bid for independence.

Martina remembered that. On an unforgettable August

21 that year, when she was eleven, she was visiting a friend in Pilsen while she played in a tennis tournament there. Russian tanks moved down the streets of Pilsen, shaking the buildings, their long guns crushing the spirit of the Czechs. The two little girls cowered indoors, over-hearing Russian soldiers shooting as people ran in the streets.

After dark when the streets were quiet, Miroslav Navratilova, the child's father, arrived in Pilsen from Prague on a motorcycle. He parked it carefully, made his way on foot to collect Martina at her friend's house, and returned with her on the machine to their home in Rev-nice, a Prague suburb.

By 1968, though, Martina was already a tennis player of great promise who had been taught from age five by her father, a bookkeeper in a tram factory. The Czech federation sent her overseas in 1973 when she was six-teen, a left-hander with an unusual style for a Euro-pean—the serve-and-volley game that is usually anathema on the slow clay of the contient.

In the United States, Bud Collins, tennis writer and television commentator, found Martina's way exciting. "No European woman since the lithe, leaping, Gallic Su-zanne Lenglen of the 1920s has played with such gusto, though Lenglen seemed a ballerina, a distinct contrast to bulldozer Navratilova," Collins wrote. He called her style bold, determined and agile.

Playing that way while growing up in Europe had not been easy. "I kept getting passed when I rushed the net," she reflected once, "but I kept coming in even though ev-erybody said I was crazy. I was losing, losing, but still I was attacking. Slowly, as I grew, I began cutting off passing shots with my volleys. My serve got stronger. I began to win. I don't have the patience to stay back on the baseline for long points in the European way."

She visited the U.S. and Canada with another player of promise, Maria Neumannova, occasionally joined for tournaments by two Czech men, Jiri Hrebec and the reigning Wimbledon champion that year, Jan Kodes. In practice with the men she showed power in her young left arm. She recalled once that when she and Neumannova travelled the women's circuit neither had much money, so they filled empty stomachs in pancake houses. Before the winter was out Martina was showing a thigh and beam far beyond her years, and her weight had topped 160. In spite of it, she moved up from qualifying ranks on the Virigina Slims circuit to a regular place in the draws.

In the summer of 1974 she showed a real flair in the French Open when she handled American clay expert Nancy Richey. Nothing in tennis is slower than the red clay of the Roland Garros Stadium in Paris. Until Chris Evert, no U.S. player could handle it better than Richey. Nonetheless, Martina serve-and-volleyed her dizzy at 6–3, 6–3.

She toured the U.S. again the next winter and her silhouette grew ever sturdier and her weight climbed to 172 pounds. Returning home was a disguised blessing; the additives in U.S. food were turning her into a blimp on hamburger row.

But a colorful blimp. Crowds took to her slam-bang game and her uninhibited ways. She quickly picked up the language, the slang and the nuances. She growled and scowled at lines calls when they went the wrong way.

The crowds dug her. Indeed, she was growing too Americanized for the taste of the federation back home, which began to curtail her travel.

"When I learned that the secret police were reporting on me to the federation I protested, but it meant nothing," she related once, frowning. "When I learned they'd said I was planning to defect, I knew I had to. It wasn't true but when they get an idea fixed in their minds they will not change it. My parents had told me if I ever felt I had to leave, not to discuss it. Just go—but make up my mind I'd never be coming back, maybe never see them or my sister Jana again."

For a time it appeared she might have waited too long. The federation decided not to allow her to play at Forest Hills in 1975. Then she was allowed to go after all. So when she got there she said she was not going back. She had decided to make the break.

"The newspapers reported I was looking for political asylum but that wasn't right," she said later. "I'm not political. I just want freedom to play tennis and I couldn't have that at home. I didn't want to leave. I miss my family badly, but then I remember how depressed I was the last time I was there. The control was tightening. I wondered if I'd get out again. There is the feeling you have no control over your own life there, no hope of getting ahead."

Kodes, a man who helped get her to Forest Hills, said she made a mistake when she defected. "We don't have maybe as much freedom as in the States but Martina would have been all right," he said. And Cyril Suk, Czech tennis administrator, called the defection "a tragedy for her and for us." She had led the Czechs to the Federation

Cup, the world event for women corresponding to the Davis Cup for men. "We would welcome Martina back, everything forgiven, any time she chose," Suk told Bud Collins in 1977.

But when Collins relayed the words of Suk and Kodes, Navratilova had a mirthless smile. "Kodes looks at it from a man's point of view, and there is more freedom for men," she told Collins. "As for going back, I know that would be bad. A man from the embassy came to see me a few days after I defected and tried to persuade me to return. He said if I waited there would be a jail sentence."

Having defected for tennis (and hamburgers) Navratilova scored two victories of importance psychologically (and continued to stuff herself). She beat Evonne Goolagong for the first time, in a Slims final at Boston, and then won the Wimbledon doubles with Evert, beating Billie Jean and Betty Stove by 6–1, 3–6, 7–5. The Wimbledon title helped her confidence even though her partner, Evert, kept beating her in singles—in the final of the French in 1975 and in the final of the Italian in 1974 and 1975.

Also, 1975 was the year she went to pieces in public at Forest Hills. She had been given a good chance to challenge Evert there, seeded back of Goolagong. In her first match she was sailing along unbothered by Janet Newberry, a sturdy Californian who dropped the first set 6–1. Then Newberry began getting the ball back and Navratilova began netting easy volleys and banging out overheads. First thing Martina knew, Newberry had the second set 6–4. And as Janet moved implacably ahead, Navratilova's aplomb began to desert her. When the Californian upended her 6–3 the sky had fallen.

"I never saw anybody so miserable, so totally out of control," said Newberry, who stood beside the seated sobbing Martina trying awkwardly to comfort her.

Perhaps more was made of the incident than was necessary. Since Navratilova had just made a life-changing decision—to cut herself off from her family and childhood friends, perhaps forever—every misstep loomed as an indication she'd made a grave mistake. Small wonder tears flowed.

What saved her as much as anything was the friendship of Sandra Haynie, the U.S. women's golf champion in 1974 who retired from the golf tour to represent pro athletes in business. Haynie was an assured and poised person thirteen years older than Navratilova and she was that much wiser in handling the exterior pressures confronting big-money athletes.

"I tried to assure her she was in the sort of slump that overtakes everybody," Haynie said of the fiery Czech. "She'd never had a bad year; as a youngster she'd won her country's singles championship three years in a row, and she'd caught on quickly in this country. When she couldn't understand her bad year I kept telling her it was normal." She was able to help her at close range; the two women shared a house on the outskirts of Dallas.

Haynie encouraged Martina to take control of her weight and her temper. She'd sit near the court; when there was a questionable call Navratilova would look at her instead of the myopic misanthrope assigned to the lines whose only mission in life obviously was to rob her blind. A gesture from Haynie would remind her to cool it.

So she climbed to second to Evert on the Slims tour in

1977, gradually taking charge of her temperament and her appetite. By fall only top players could handle her. She lost four straight matches to Billie Jean, who came back from a third operation on a knee and won all four of those tournaments. Billie Jean, like Evert, was one of Navratilova's close friends on the tour, helping her adjust to the travel, offering advice. Still, both kept wiping the court with her in competition most of the time.

But early in 1978 in Houston Navratilova got King out of her system. Billie Jean laced the left-hander 6–1 in the first set but Martina stayed calm, got her game going, and swept the next two sets 6–2, 6–2.

From there, she was a terror. She won seven straight Slims tournaments and piled in money as fast as she could swing her left arm. In the absence of Evert, who took a four-month holiday to recharge young but worn batteries, Navratilova won thirty-seven successive matches, a Slims record, losing only six sets. As her confidence swelled, her game steadied. She expected to have an argument from Goolagong who had been out for a year having a baby but who had marked her comeback by winning four tournaments in a row on Australian grass in the late fall. But in the U.S. Goolagong had difficulty on indoor Sporteze surfaces, and foot and leg injuries hampered her.

Still, the dancing Aussie was in pretty good shape when the women assembled at Oakland in April for the Slims championships, marking the end of the annual three-months winter tour. She and Navratilova swept into the final impressively. It was a big match for the Czech who had to convince herself she'd really finally got control of her volatile emotions. She proved it too, doing wonders in outduelling Goolagong. Of course, Evert wasn't present. Coming off her holiday, she didn't compete often enough to qualify for the championship wrapup. Navratilova's transformation extended to her relations with the hard-thinking newshounds. Often she'd scorned the penetrating questions ("Are you glad you won, Martina?") but in the spring of 1978 she was the one reminding reporters that Evert was sunning herself in Florida. "I am No. 1 only if Chris is away. When she comes back, we'll see."

They met in England at Eastbourne in a June tournament leading to Wimbledon, a two-hour ten-minute drama described by some as worthy of a Wimbledon classic. Navratilova won in thirty-six all-out games by 6–4, 4–6, 9–7. "Even the Centre Court aura of Wimbledon will be extended to surpass the technical brilliance and emotional turnabouts that highlighted the match," Neil Amdur wrote in the *New York Times*. It was only the fourth of twenty-four matches that Navratilova had handled Evert.

"Technically she's the same player," was Evert's assessment. "Now she doesn't get as flustered as she used to." Still, it was just the fourth tournament of the year for Evert; only passing significance was attached to it for the forthcoming Wimbledon. The bookies made Chris the solid choice.

Centre Court tested all of Navratilova's skills and emotions and, as it turned out, she surmounted the tests with honors on the closing Wednesday and Friday of Wimbledon's celebrated fortnight, scoring in struggles. The first was over Goolagong in the semifinal and the other from Evert in the traditional Friday final. Her match with the

Australian was ultimately easy at 2–6, 6–4, 6–4 because Evonne had an ankle injury that inhibited her through the match and hobbled her in the last four games.

Goolagong played so fluently in the first set that, in the words of Rex Bellamy in the London *Times*, "Somebody should have been playing New Orleans jazz off-stage." She ran off four games with flowing improvisations. But as Bellamy also noted, "Miss Navratilova is now mature enough to tolerate adversity without being overwhelmed by it. She no longer behaves as if hostile invisible forces are moving the lines about and changing the height of the net."

So Martina was able to respond to Goolagong's opening flow by lifting her game and winning the second set. In the clincher Evonne hit a forehand lob to hold her service for a 4–3 lead, but as she hit the ball she yelped in such pain that all of the fourteen thousand surrounding the players could hear her cry. She grasped her left leg, head bowed, then limped to the umpire's chair, wiping away tears.

Martina didn't want to take advantage of a crippled player but was aware she risked defeat if she didn't. She made it mercifully quick. She lost only four points in running out the last three games.

So now she was facing Evert in the final, Evert's fourth appearance there in seven years, a young woman who had never been beaten before the semifinal—and this was supposedly a player whose eminence was confined to clay. They divided the first two sets. Evert won the opener 6–2, taking four consecutive games to do so. Then Navratilova raised her sights a notch and won the second 6–4, and hopped away to a 2–0 lead in the third.

Then Evert, two years older and a two-time Wimbledon champion, looked in the right position to relegate Navratilova to the also-ran role once more; Chris ran off four games in a row. This assuredly was the time for Martina to find a chair to sit upon for a good long cry. The old Navratilova might well have, but that youngster had changed her address. This one evened the match with firepower off the ground and at the net, attacking every ball.

Evert held off the tide for a moment, moving in front on her own service 5–4. "Suddenly," Rex Bellamy wrote, "Miss Navratilova was overwhelmingly the stronger. There were booming noises as her racquet met the ball. But now she is much more than a thumper. She would not have won but for her competitive resilience, her courage in adversity, her ability to play her finest tennis when the stakes were highest." She won the set 7–5 and with it the match. Naturally, she cried—this time for joy.

# INDEX

# INDEX

## ABOUT THE AUTHOR

TRENT FRAYNE of the *Toronto Sun* is one of Canada's top columnists and winner of that country's 1976 National Newspaper Award for sports writing. A life-long tennis enthusiast, he is the author of many successful books including *Famous Hockey Players* and *Famous Tennis Players,* which covers the men.